Quilting the Garden

Garden Glow

BARB ADAMS

Cottage Garden

ALMA ALLEN

Quilting the Garden

by Barb Adams,
Alma Allen &
Ricki Creamer

QUILTING THE GARDEN

By Barb Adams, Alma Allen and Ricki Creamer

Editor : Edie McGinnis
Copy Editor: Judy Pearlstein
Design : Kelly Ludwig
Production Assistant: Jo Ann Groves
Photography: Krissy Krausser, Rebecca Friend-Jimenez
and Bill Krzyzanowski

Published by Kansas City Star Books
1729 Grand Blvd., Kansas City, Missouri, 64108

ISBN: 0-9754804-1-3

First edition

Printed in the United States of America by
Walsworth Publishing Co.

To order copies, call StarInfo (816-234-4636)
www.PickleDish.com

Red Cedar Country Gardens
7895 W. 183rd Street
Stilwell, Kansas 66085
913-897-2286
redcedargardens@aol.com

TABLE OF CONTENTS

Quilting the Garden - Introduction

Quilters are natural gardeners! A walk through any quilt show is proof enough. Our love of nature is stitched into every quilt, be it through the appliqué or the quilting stitch embedded throughout the layers of fabric and batting. Our gardens bloom with bright batiks, subtle plaids and a variety of prints. We highlight and reflect nature with a passion. As Barb and I began to design these blocks, we felt that each of our fabric container gardens could be accompanied with the real thing.

We invited Ricki Creamer of Red Cedar Country Gardens to contribute her talents. The quiet beauty of her country garden is a favorite place for gardeners to take classes, purchase plants and see new ideas. Her container gardens are designed to draw you into their beauty. Her choice of plants and containers are fresh and inviting. She graciously agreed to join our book endeavor. As Barb and I highlight each block of the featured quilt, Ricki provides an idea for a seasonal container garden for your outdoor living space.

Quilters know that combining foliage and flowers which reflect and enhance each other brings joy and pleasure. Our fabric knowledge of pattern, texture, design and color is translated easily to container gardening. We realize the visual impact container gardens can add to our outdoor living spaces. Containers can fill empty areas, add visual height, frame our outdoor spaces and focus our attention to the garden. Container gardens offer a simple opportunity to experiment with color and texture. Regardless of your space, there is always room for a container of plants! Magic and wonder can be easily added to your outside living space by these small, contained gardens which decorate our spaces where we relax, entertain and enjoy nature.

The design strategy, both for container gardens and for our appliquéd blocks, is the same. Choose a plant for the centerpiece, add a couple of plants that enhance and reflect the centerpiece, include a filler plant to cover the bare spots and soften and break up the lines of the container with a trailing plant.

This book would not have been possible without the contribution of many. We owe much to the following people:

The design ideas and sewing skills of Jean Stanclift, Leona Adams and Lynn Droege have enhanced each project. Jeanne Zyck, Pamela Mayfield and Lori Kukuk designed the quilting for our quilt tops. Pam Mayfield added her touch to a quilt design using four of the featured quilt blocks. Sherry Carey's embroidery stitches give our quilt embellished style.

Krissy Krauser and Rebecca Friend-Jimenez, *The Kansas City Star* photographers, give us an intimate view of the container gardens. Their close-up shots of the flowers illustrate the true wonder of the garden.

Bill Krzyzanowski's photography brings the quilts and projects into clear view. His lighting and angle of view reflect his careful consideration of each photograph.

Kelly Ludwig's beautiful book design binds our efforts into a compelling format. Her vision of the book reflects our theme.

Eric Craven has illustrated the diagrams and patterns for the book. His clear and quick understanding have been essential to our project.

Judy Pearlstein and Edie McGinnis bring clear concise instructions through their editing skills.

Many thanks go to our editor Edie McGinnis of Kansas City Star Books! She orchestrated the efforts of all, which was no small task.

Finally, thanks belong to you for allowing us to share these container gardens and quilt patterns with you. We hope your gardens, whether quilted or grown in containers, continue to reveal their beauty and wonder and bring you hours of pleasure! Enjoy!

Hand Applique Instructions

■ Make templates of the appliqué shapes with plastic template material. Do not add any seam allowance to these plastic shapes.

■ Trace around the plastic templates on the right side of your fabric. Use a marking pencil that will show up on your fabric. This drawn line indicates your seam line. To cut reversed pieces, flip the plastic template over and trace the reversed shape to the right side of your fabric.

■ Cut out the fabric shapes, now adding a 1/8" - 1/4" seam allowance.

■ Fold the background fabric in half vertically and horizontally. Finger-press the folds. Open the fabric.

■ To help achieve exact placement of the design, trace the design to tracing paper. Place the tracing paper over the background block. Lift the paper up and place the appliqué shape on the background. Lower the tracing paper to check for correct placement. The pattern layout is available for each of the featured quilt blocks. They are printed at 40% of the original size. To get the correct block size, enlarge the drawings to 250% on a copy machine.

■ Center the design on the background block using the fold lines or tracing paper as a guide.

■ Baste the shapes into place on the background block with glue stick or appliqué pins. Larger shapes require basting stitches to hold the shapes in place securely.

■ Use thread that matches your appliqué piece, not the background. Use a two-ply, cotton thread that is 50 or 60 weight.

■ Cut the thread length about 12"-15". Longer lengths of thread may become worn and break as you stitch.

■ For concave curves (curves that go in) clip to the seam line, then turn under the seam allowance. This will allow the fabric to lie flat. Convex curves, or curves that go out, do not require clipping.

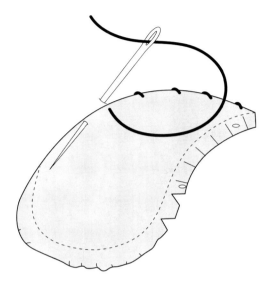

■ Sew the pieces that "tuck-under" another piece first. For example, sew the stems first. Next, sew the flower or leaf that covers the end of the stem.

■ Using the point and edge of your needle, turn under the fabric on the drawn seam line and appliqué the shape to the background fabric. Try to achieve about 7-9 stitches per inch.

Winter Haven

Winter Haven

As winter settles in, the days become shorter. With less daylight and colder weather, it's harder to venture into the garden. Welcome nature into your garden by embracing the winter season with greenery and berries. Ricki Creamer, of Red Cedar Country Gardens, uses an antique, cast-stone watering trough, planted with flowers in the summer but transformed in the winter to celebrate the colder season. Lure nature back into your garden and heart with this winter haven.

A birdbath near a viewing window will work well for Ricki's idea. Start by placing a twig wreath in the base of your dry birdbath. Next, gather greens of all kinds. Boxwood, cedar, holly and pine branches offer a variety of textures and scents. Arrange this greenery around the wreath. Add berry branches, moss and pine cones for a hint of the forest. The freshness of the natural materials is perfect for the winter garden. In the center of the wreath, add an urn or a large shallow container filled with birdseed to welcome birds into your garden. As you gaze outside, the connection with greenery and visiting birds is restorative.

If you're planning to entertain, nestle candles into the birdseed for an inviting scene as guests arrive at your home in the evening.

Bring extra greenery inside to add the fresh scent of pine to your home. Place evergreen boughs on your mantle and twine them around stair rails. Even a small sprig of a pine branch in a soap dish is a daily reminder of your garden.

Small, cut pine trees can be "planted" in containers. Using a plastic pot as a liner, fill with moist sand and firmly slide the tree trunk into the sand. Placed outside on your deck or front porch, the trees stay green and fresh for a month if you keep the sand moist. They are also perfect inside, adding the fresh and natural scent of nature to your home. Pictured above are three cut pines shown "planted" into the container.

❀❀ Winter Haven - Block One ❀❀

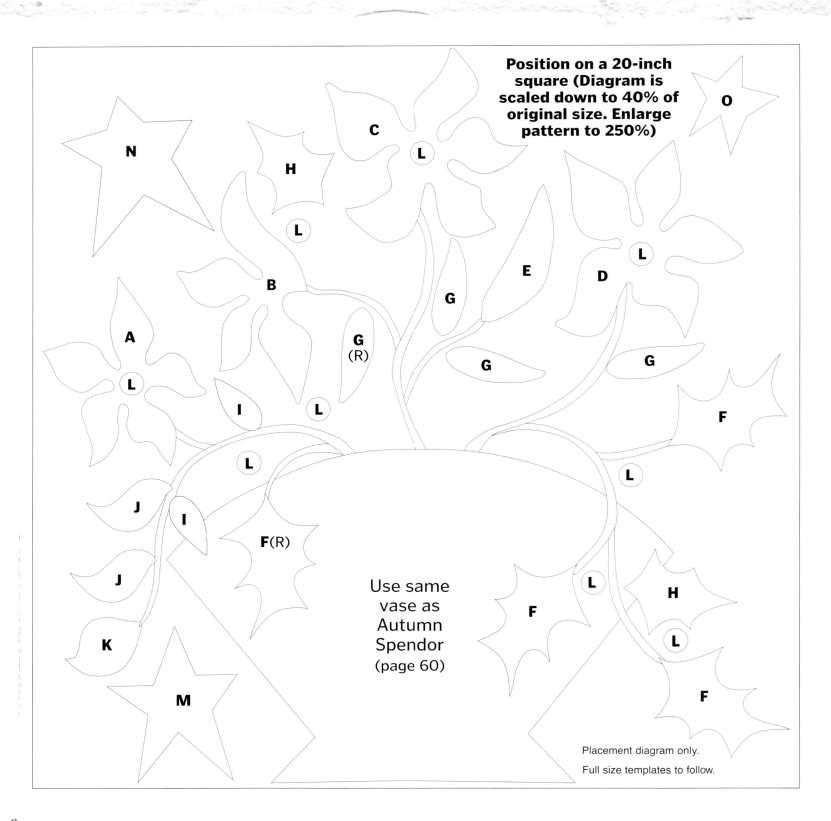

Position on a 20-inch square (Diagram is scaled down to 40% of original size. Enlarge pattern to 250%)

Use same vase as Autumn Spendor (page 60)

Placement diagram only.

Full size templates to follow.

8

BLOCK INSTRUCTIONS

Our winter block features poinsettia blooms, holly leaves and berries.

- Cut the background block 20 1/2" x 20 1/2".

- Make 1/4" bias tape for flower and vine stems.

- Make the appliqué templates.

- Trace around the templates on the right side of your fabric for needle-turn appliqué. Refer to the picture to help with color choice.

- Cut out the shapes, adding your seam allowance.

- Follow the appliqué instructions on page 4 and sew the pieces to your background block.

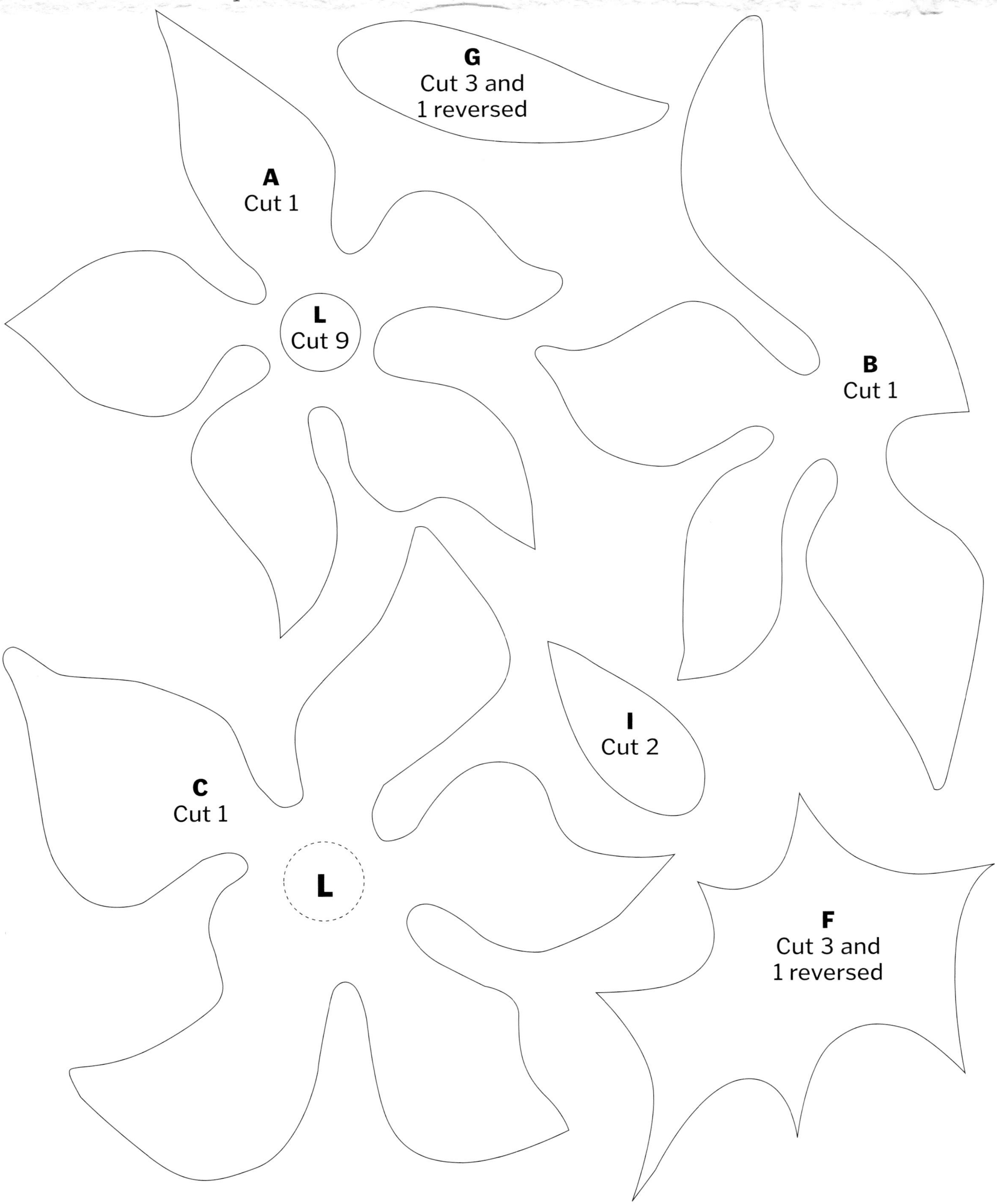

G
Cut 3 and
1 reversed

A
Cut 1

L
Cut 9

B
Cut 1

C
Cut 1

I
Cut 2

L

F
Cut 3 and
1 reversed

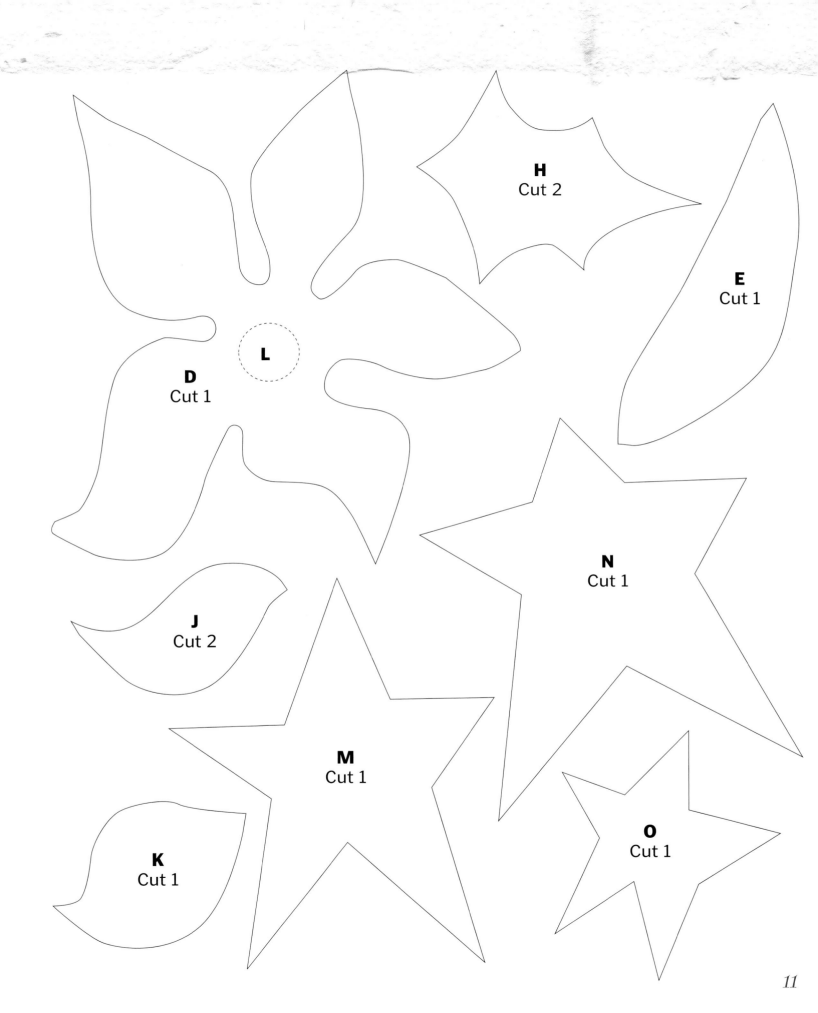

H
Cut 2

E
Cut 1

D
Cut 1

L

N
Cut 1

J
Cut 2

M
Cut 1

O
Cut 1

K
Cut 1

11

Winter Bloom

Winter Bloom

A visit to Red Cedar Country Gardens is a treat even in the depths of winter! With snow on the ground and the world white, Ricki brings the color and freshness of the garden into her home.

A woven wire basket reveals tightly packed green sheet moss, the base of this winter basket. To plant this basket, you will need: one bag of sheet moss, potting soil, several forced paperwhite bulbs, an amaryllis just beginning to bloom, a golden cypress, a cyclamen plant and several pine branches.

Dip the sheet moss in water for a couple of seconds. Drain the moss of excess water. Thickly line the base and sides of the basket with the damp sheet moss. Make sure there are no open spaces between the pieces of sheet moss. Add potting soil to fill the basket. Refer to the diagram and set the plants into the potting soil. When the flowers are planted, add pieces of sheet moss to cover the potting soil.

Press the cut ends of fresh pine branches into the soil for extra greenery around the base of the paperwhites and amaryllis. The softness of the pine needles adds a place to hide a resting bird or small garden ornament. This fresh container garden is the perfect winter centerpiece filling your home with the color and scent of winter.

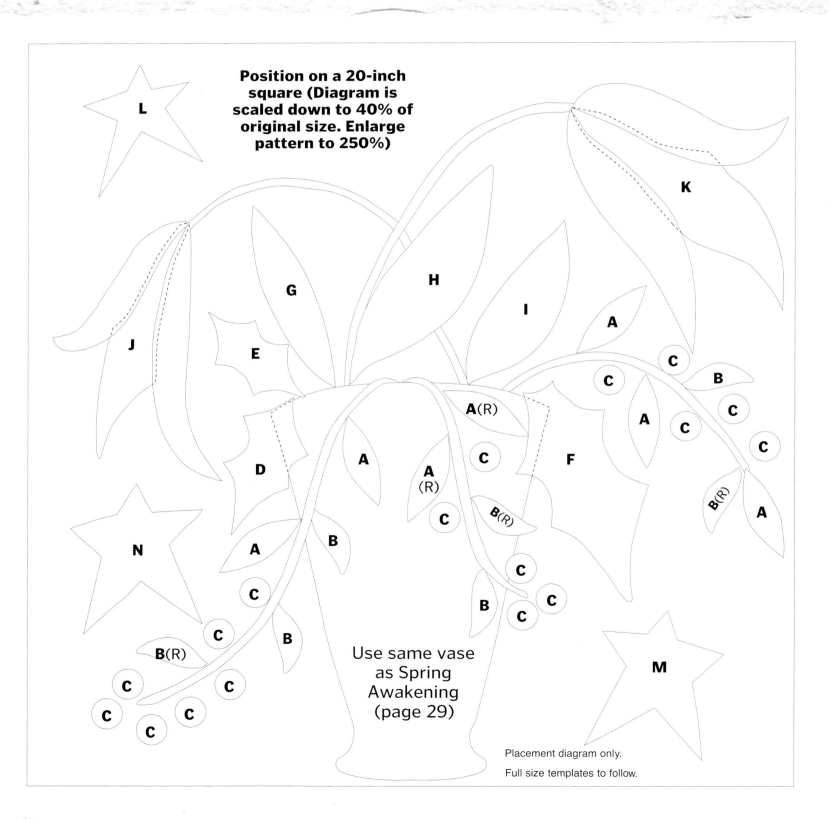

Position on a 20-inch square (Diagram is scaled down to 40% of original size. Enlarge pattern to 250%)

L

K

J

G

H

I

A

E

C

C

B

A(R)

C

C

A

C

F

C

D

A

A
(R)

C

B(R)

A

C

B

B(R)

C

N

A

C

B

C

C

C

Use same vase as Spring Awakening (page 29)

M

C

B(R)

C

C

C

C

Placement diagram only.

Full size templates to follow.

Our winter block features amaryllis blooms, holly leaves and berries.

BLOCK INSTRUCTIONS

- Cut the background block 20 1/2" x 20 1/2".

- Make 1/4" bias tape for flower and vine stems.

- Make the appliqué templates.

- Trace around the templates on the right side of your fabric for needle-turn appliqué. Refer to the picture to help with color choice.

- Cut out the shapes, adding your seam allowance.

- Follow the appliqué instructions on page 4 and sew the pieces to your background block.

TWIGS

CUT PINE BRANCHES

AMARYLLIS

CYCLAMEN

GOLDEN CYPRESS

PAPERWHITES

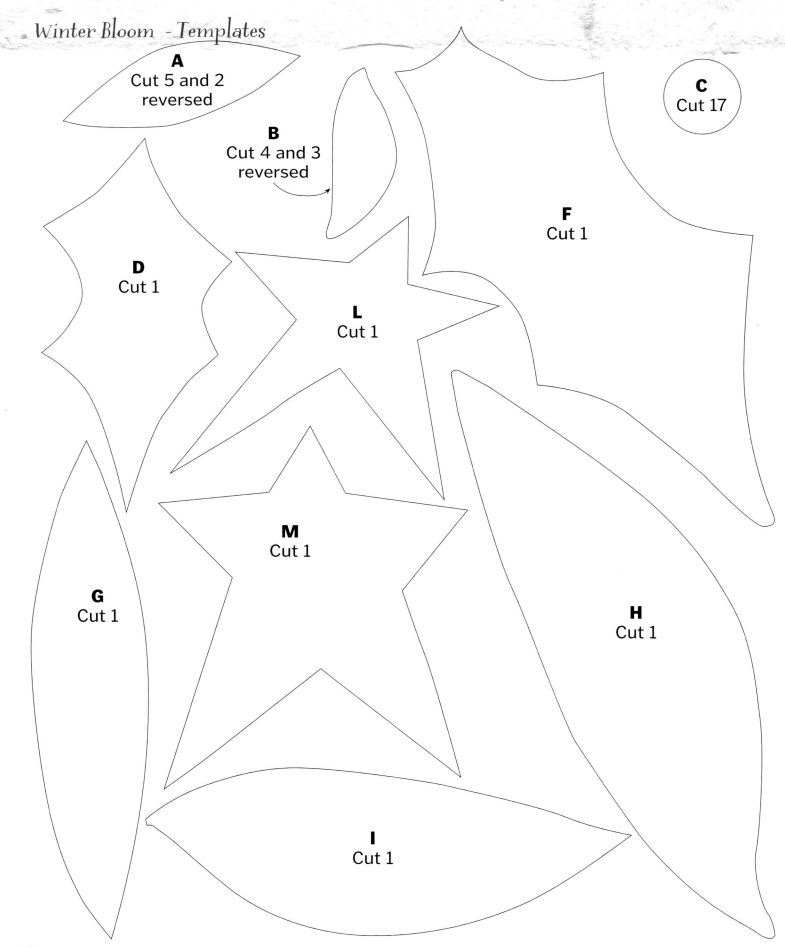

A
Cut 5 and 2 reversed

B
Cut 4 and 3 reversed

C
Cut 17

D
Cut 1

F
Cut 1

L
Cut 1

M
Cut 1

G
Cut 1

H
Cut 1

I
Cut 1

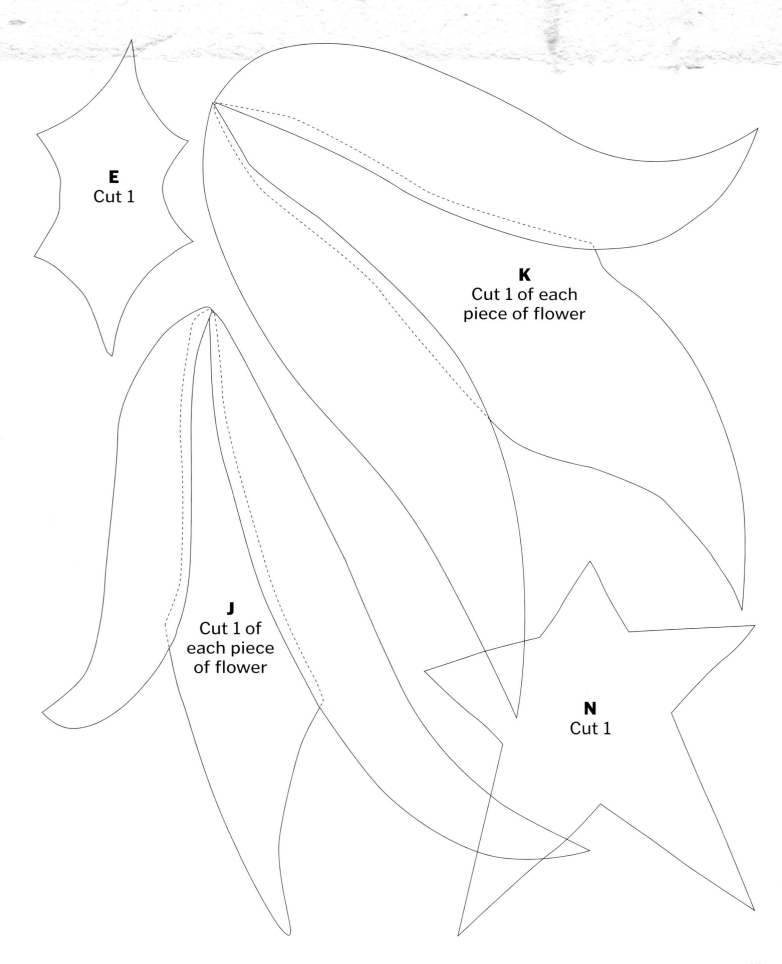

E
Cut 1

K
Cut 1 of each
piece of flower

J
Cut 1 of
each piece
of flower

N
Cut 1

Hearts of Spring

Hearts of Spring

Container gardens are a fun way to experiment with plant combinations. Adding a fresh touch of early bloom to your containers brings the very heart of spring to your garden. This one uses only white flowers. The small dove accentuates the color schemes. This garden will like morning sun with afternoon shade and will continue to bloom through June.

The texture of the leaves adds much to this garden. When choosing plants for a container garden, Ricki looks for a variety of leaf shapes to add texture. She looks for an upright plant and for a plant that drapes over the side of the container. A "filler" plant is important for each container. The filler plant in this container is sweet alyssum. It spreads out and fills any open spaces. After the plants have been set into the potting soil, tuck sheet moss around each plant to cover the bare spots of soil. The sheet moss gives the container garden a finished look and helps protect from moisture loss during the heat of the day.

From the beginning of the season, container gardens should look full and lush. With annuals having such a short season of growth, more is better. Feeding with an organic plant food and careful attention to water needs, keeps these containers in bright spring color. Fill and pack are the key words here!

The plants in this all white container garden are: white primrose, gerber daisy, bacopa and sweet alyssum. The small dove brings a touch of spring.

◎ Hearts of Spring - Block Three ◎

Position on a 20-inch square (Diagram is scaled down to 40% of original size. Enlarge pattern to 250%

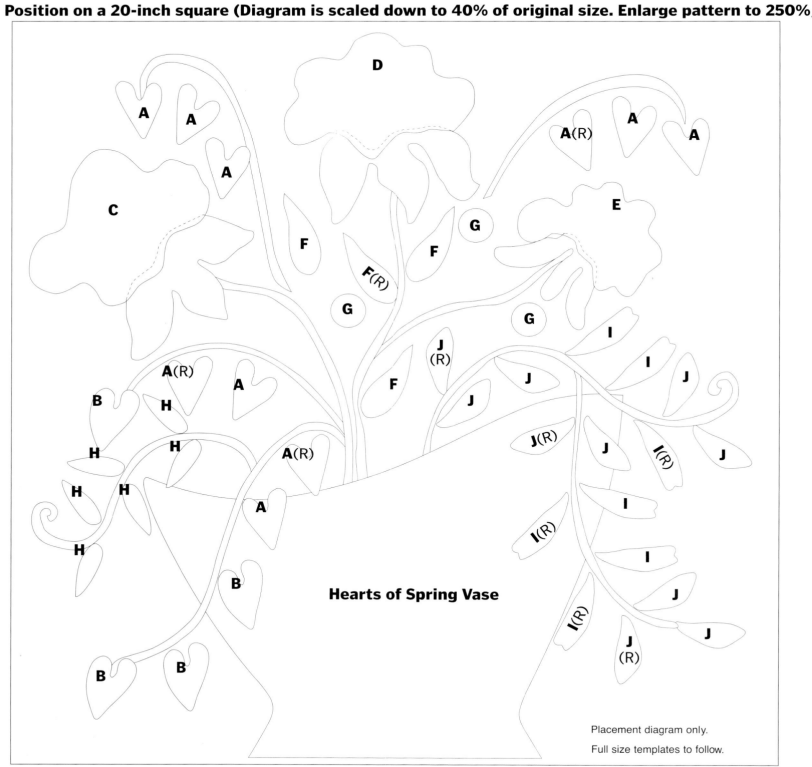

Hearts of Spring Vase

Placement diagram only.

Full size templates to follow.

Our spring block contains bleeding hearts and peonies. Many varieties of peonies are available. Ricki sells cut peony flowers by the dozens in the spring and they make wonderful bouquets. Each bouquet contains a mixture of peony varieties and is a wonder to behold! Their sweet smell and lush bloom are a joy.

BLOCK INSTRUCTIONS

- Cut the background block 20 1/2" x 20 1/2".

- Make 1/4" bias tape for flower and vine stems.

- Make the appliqué templates.

- Trace around the templates on the right side of your fabric for needle-turn appliqué. Refer to the picture to help with color choice.

- Cut out the shapes, adding your seam allowance.

- Follow the appliqué instructions on page 4 and sew the pieces to your background block.

SWEET ALYSSUM

SWEET ALYSSUM

BACOPA
WHITE PRIMROSE

GERBER DAISY

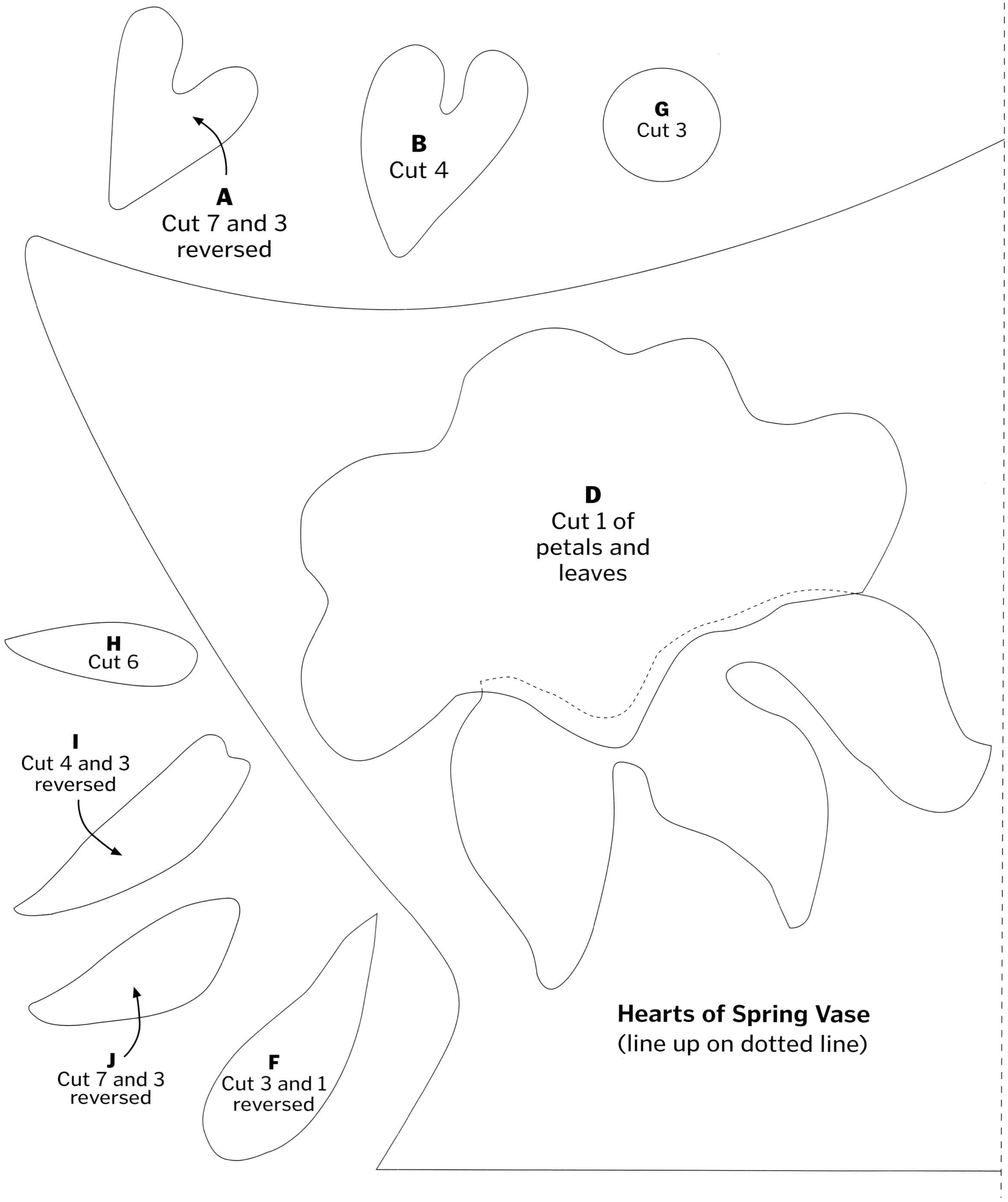

A
Cut 7 and 3
reversed

B
Cut 4

G
Cut 3

D
Cut 1 of
petals and
leaves

H
Cut 6

I
Cut 4 and 3
reversed

J
Cut 7 and 3
reversed

F
Cut 3 and 1
reversed

Hearts of Spring Vase
(line up on dotted line)

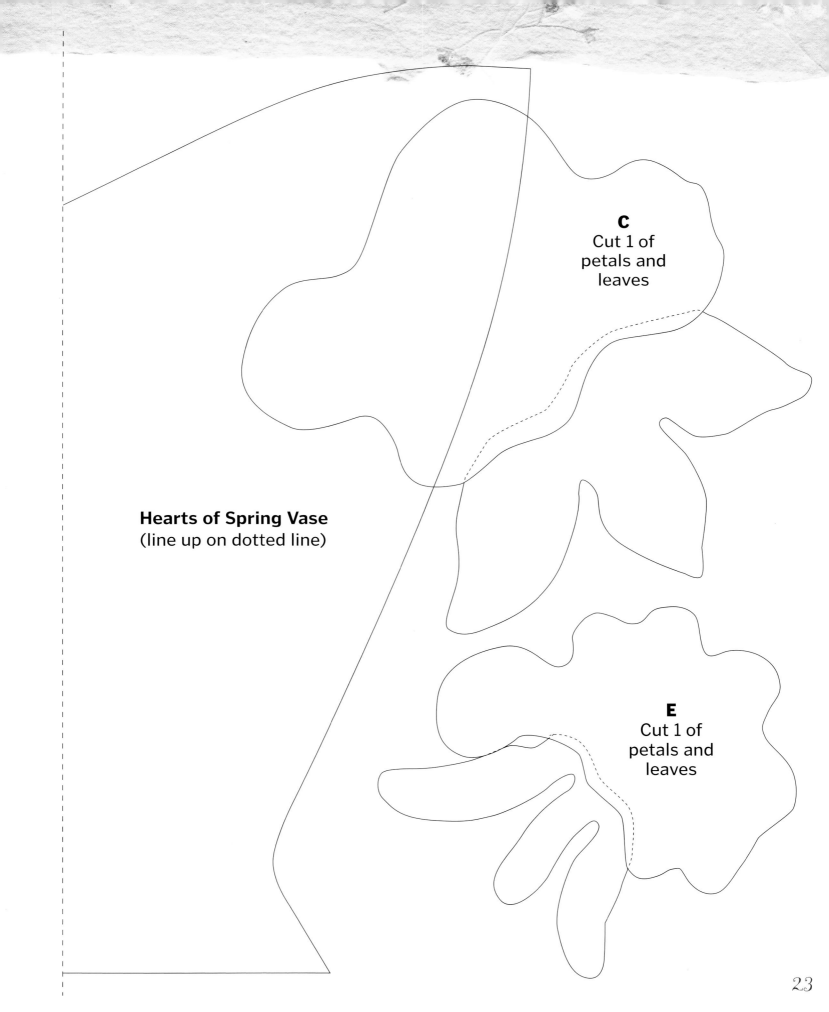

C
Cut 1 of
petals and
leaves

Hearts of Spring Vase
(line up on dotted line)

E
Cut 1 of
petals and
leaves

Spring Awakening

Spring Awakening

As bright dappled light filters through the trees in the garden, we are welcomed by a container of spring flowers. In the early spring, Ricki believes the garden should be highlighted, so she places container gardens among her flower beds. As the perennial flower beds are not in full bloom early in the spring, the container garden brings the welcome touches of color and visual height until the perennials are at their best.

Pansies are often used for spring and fall plantings. Adding a combination of fairy bouquets (better known as linaria) and osteospermum flowers gives the pansies an updated fresh look. Tucked under the pansies is a bit of scotch moss in bloom. The delicate white flowers invite a garden visitor closer to inspect the bloom and touch the velvet moss. Growing at the base of the urn are fresh shoots of variegated liriope and sweet mini-daffodils.

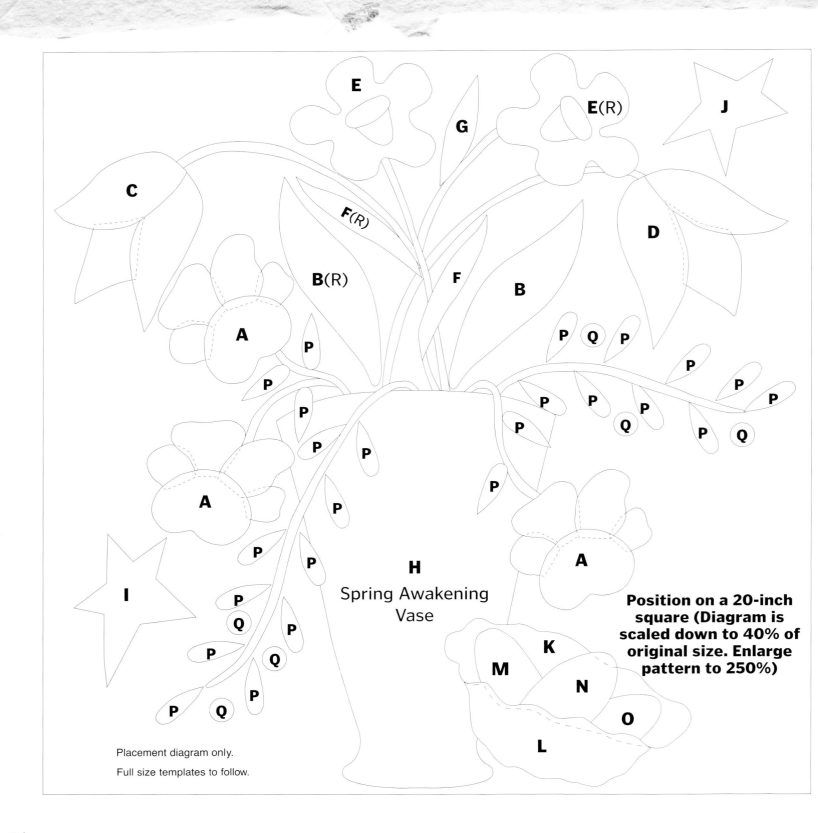

Spring Awakening
Vase

Position on a 20-inch
square (Diagram is
scaled down to 40% of
original size. Enlarge
pattern to 250%)

Placement diagram only.

Full size templates to follow.

This spring block contains daffodils and tulips, some of our favorite spring flowers. Each spring a robin's nest is invariably dislodged from a tree by a rain storm. These fallen nests are added to my container gardens. I can't bear to toss them away!

BLOCK INSTRUCTIONS

▪ Cut the background block 20 1/2" x 20 1/2".

▪ Make 1/4" bias tape for flower and vine stems.

▪ Make the appliqué templates.

▪ Trace around the templates on the right side of your fabric for needle-turn appliqué. Refer to the picture to help with color choice.

▪ Cut out the shapes, adding your seam allowance.

▪ Follow the appliqué instructions on page 4 and sew the pieces to your background block.

LIRIOPE
VARIEGATED

PANSIES

SCOTCH MOSS

OSTEOSPURMUM

MINI-
DAFFODIL

PANSIES

LINARIA

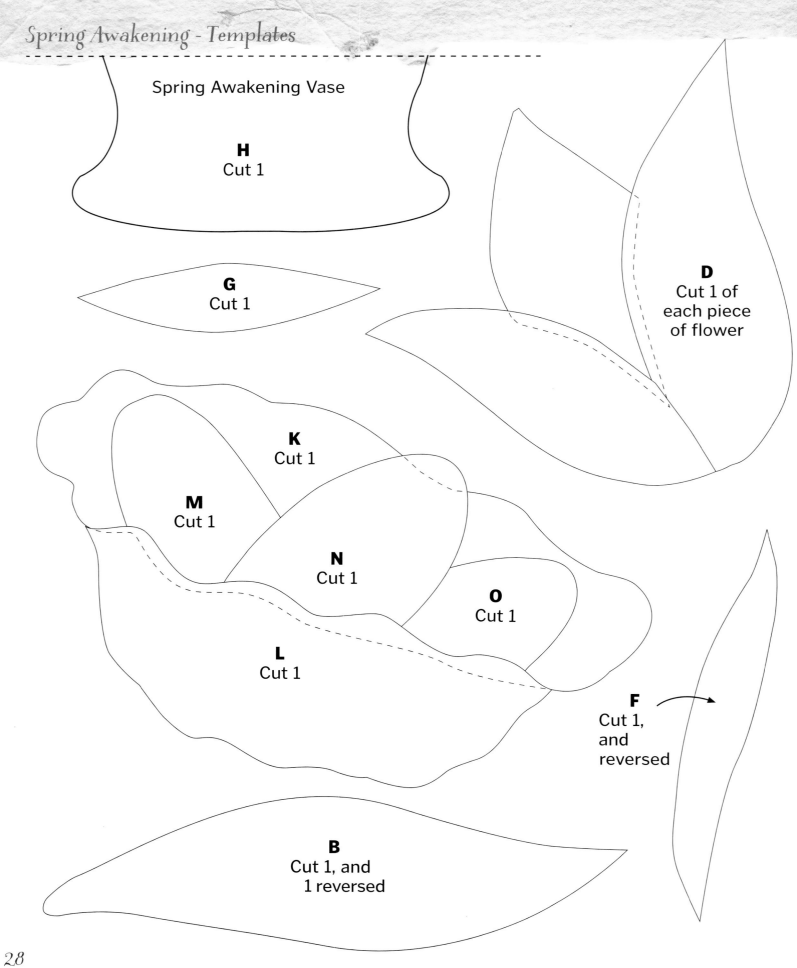

Spring Awakening Vase

H
Cut 1

G
Cut 1

D
Cut 1 of
each piece
of flower

K
Cut 1

M
Cut 1

N
Cut 1

O
Cut 1

L
Cut 1

F
Cut 1,
and
reversed

B
Cut 1, and
1 reversed

28

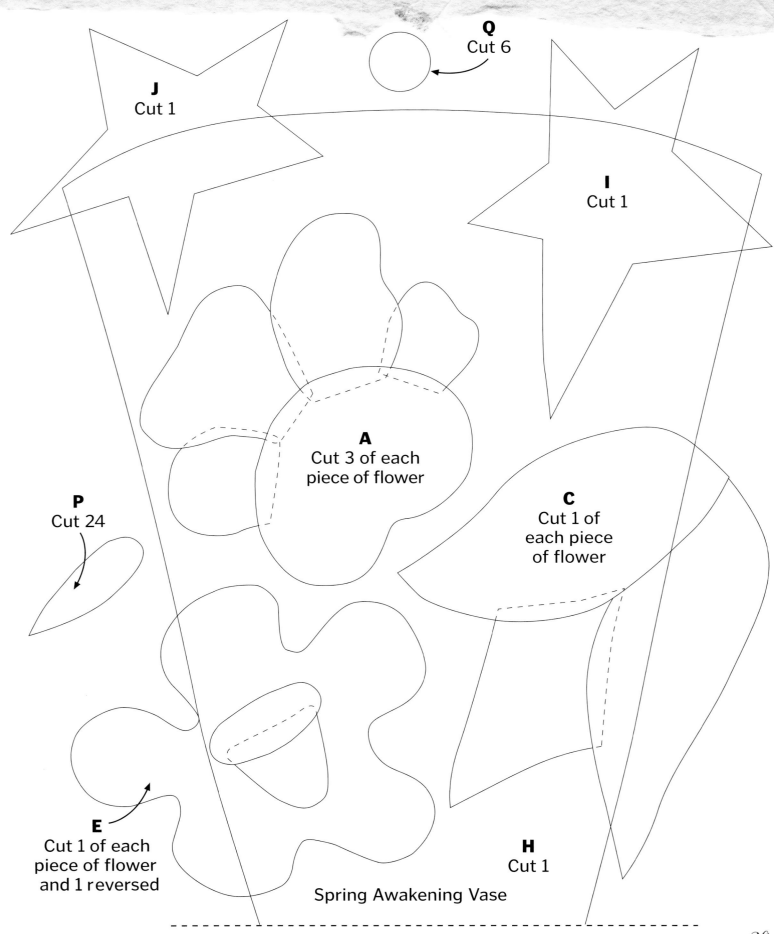

J
Cut 1

Q
Cut 6

I
Cut 1

A
Cut 3 of each
piece of flower

C
Cut 1 of
each piece
of flower

P
Cut 24

E
Cut 1 of each
piece of flower
and 1 reversed

H
Cut 1

Spring Awakening Vase

Pleasures of Summer

Pleasures of Summer

A dd style to your patio with this French country planter! The iron work of this planter lends a classic touch to the back wall of Ricki's patio. This simple but elegant planter offers a visual backdrop for the lush bloom of these brilliant flowers.

Wall planters bring container gardens to a new height. At this intimate eye level, we feel connected to the garden. This idea is also perfect for balconies where lack of space is an issue. The green of the leaves is refreshing, decorating the patio for reading, quiet moments and informal entertaining.

The flowers in this summer planter will grow best in sunlight. Summer light is so intense that the bright colors "pop" in the full sun while pastel shades of flowers tend to fade away. The bright bloom of the red cape daisy enhances the purple angelonia and 'Homestead' purple verbena. The lime geranium leaf adds that special chartreuse color to the planting. The soft, silvery gray-green foliage of the trailing licorice plant feathers the edges of the planter.

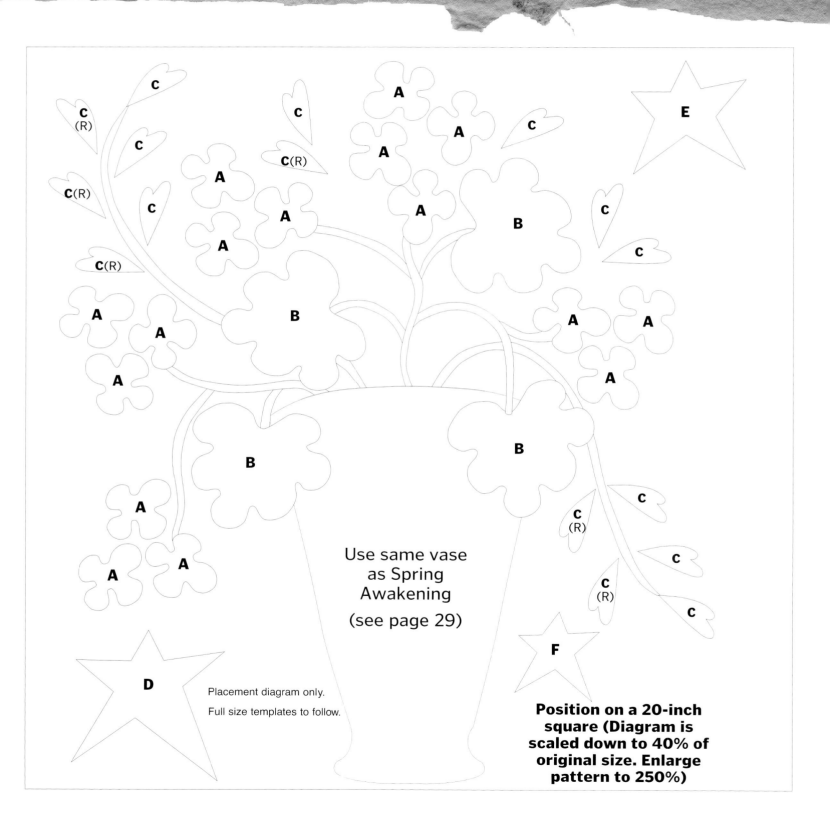

C
C(R)
C
C(R)
C(R)
A
A
A
A
C
C
C(R)
A
A
A
A
A
A
A
A
A
B
A
A
B
A
A
A
A
A
A
A
C
B
C
C(R)
E
B
A
A
A
A
B
C
C(R)
C
C

Use same vase
as Spring
Awakening
(see page 29)

F

D

Placement diagram only.

Full size templates to follow.

**Position on a 20-inch
square (Diagram is
scaled down to 40% of
original size. Enlarge
pattern to 250%)**

Our quilted geranium blooms with summer exuberance! When choosing plants for your container garden, consider the scented-leaf geranium. Although its bloom is less dramatic than other geraniums, it makes up for it by providing the sensual pleasure of its aroma when you rub its leaves. From fruity scents of lemon and orange to floral scents of rose, the scented geraniums leave a lasting remembrance on the hands of the gardener.

BLOCK INSTRUCTIONS

▨ Cut the background block 20 1/2" x 20 1/2".

▨ Make 1/4" bias tape for flower and vine stems.

▨ Make the appliqué templates.

▨ Trace around the templates on the right side of your fabric for needle-turn appliqué. Refer to the picture to help with color choice.

▨ Cut out the shapes, adding your seam allowance.

▨ Follow the appliqué instructions on page 4 and sew the pieces to your background block.

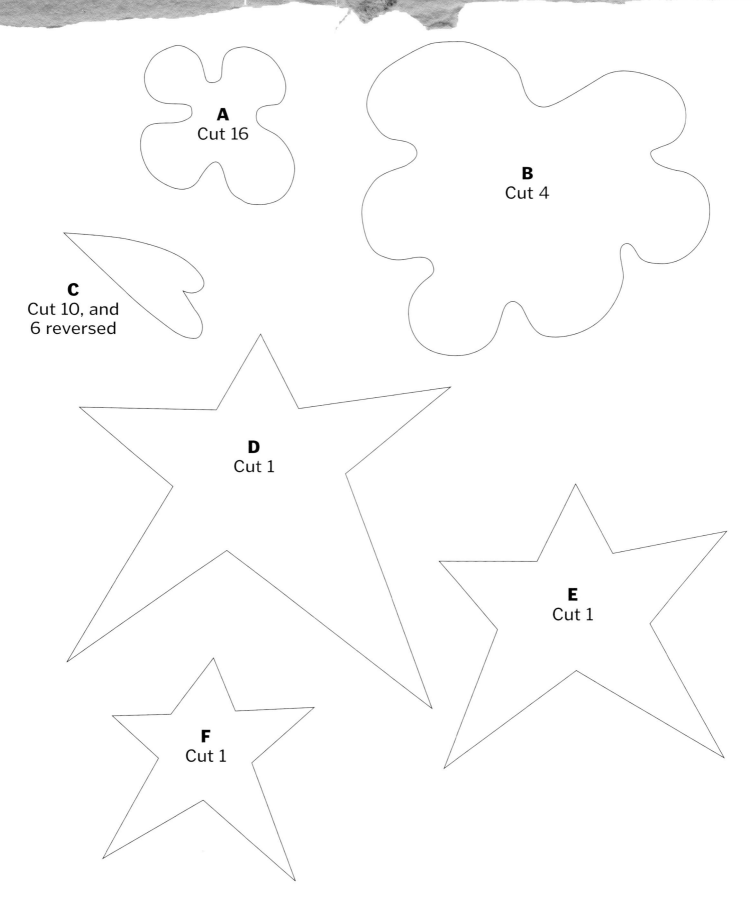

A
Cut 16

B
Cut 4

C
Cut 10, and
6 reversed

D
Cut 1

E
Cut 1

F
Cut 1

PURPLE
ANGELONIA

'CRYSTAL PALACE GEM'
VARIEGATED GERANIUM

'SILVER LACE'
DUSTY MILLER

'HOMESTEAD'
PURPLE VERBENA

HELICHRYSUM

RUSTIC ORANGE
COLEUS

RED CAPE DAISY
ARGYRANTHEMUM

Summer Herbs

Summer Herbs

This hanging iron trough is perfect for a privacy fence. By raising this container to eye level, the fence is changed from a blank wall into a source of terrific visual interest. The addition of the herb plaque on the fence illustrates how fencing can be used as the walls of the garden and can be decorated just like the interior walls of your home. The plaque becomes a "painting" enhancing the planting below it. Two small, pot trellises are placed in the trough to add height and symmetry. Trailing plants soften the fence and whimsical flowers add color and scent to the wall.

When attaching these troughs or any container to your fence or garden walls, make certain they are secured well. The plants and the weight of the soil when watered, can become extremely heavy. These open containers also dry out easily, so they may need to be watered daily in the summer heat.

This hanging trough requires three bags of sheet moss, potting soil, two lamb's ear plants, two dwarf trailing snapdragon plants, two mixed primrose plants, two each of pink and purple linaria, three violas and two scotch moss plants.

Dip the sheet moss in the water for a couple of seconds. Drain the moss of excess water. Thickly line the base and sides of the trough with this damp sheet moss. Make sure there are no open spaces between the pieces of sheet moss. Add potting soil to fill the trough. Refer to the diagram and place the plants into the potting soil. When the flowers are planted, add pieces of sheet moss to cover the potting soil.

As June approaches, Ricki replaces the linaria, viola and primroses with golden sage, silver-edged thyme, blue-green chives, purple-leafed peppers and scented geraniums for a summer garden of herbal delight.

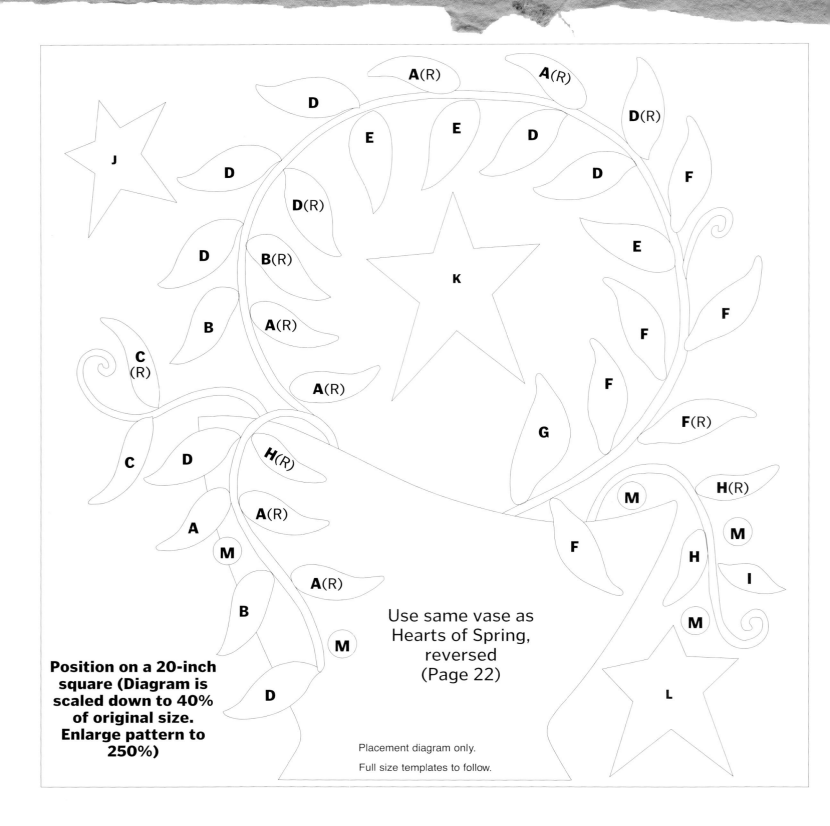

A(R) A(R)
D
D(R)
J
E E D
D
D
F
D(R)
E
D B(R)
K
B A(R)
F
F
C (R)
F
A(R)
F(R)
G
C D H(R)
M H(R)
M
A(R)
F H M
A I
M
A(R)
B M

Use same vase as
Hearts of Spring,
reversed
(Page 22)

**Position on a 20-inch
square (Diagram is
scaled down to 40%
of original size.
Enlarge pattern to
250%)**

D

L

Placement diagram only.

Full size templates to follow.

Our block features an herb topiary. Scented geraniums, rosemary and dwarf myrtle are excellent choices for topiaries.

BLOCK INSTRUCTIONS

- Cut the background block 20 1/2" x 20 1/2".

- Make 1/4" bias tape for flower and vine stems.

- Make the appliqué templates.

- Trace around the templates on the right side of your fabric for needle-turn appliqué. Refer to the picture to help with color choice.

- Cut out the shapes, adding your seam allowance.

- Follow the appliqué instructions on page 4 and sew the pieces to your background block.

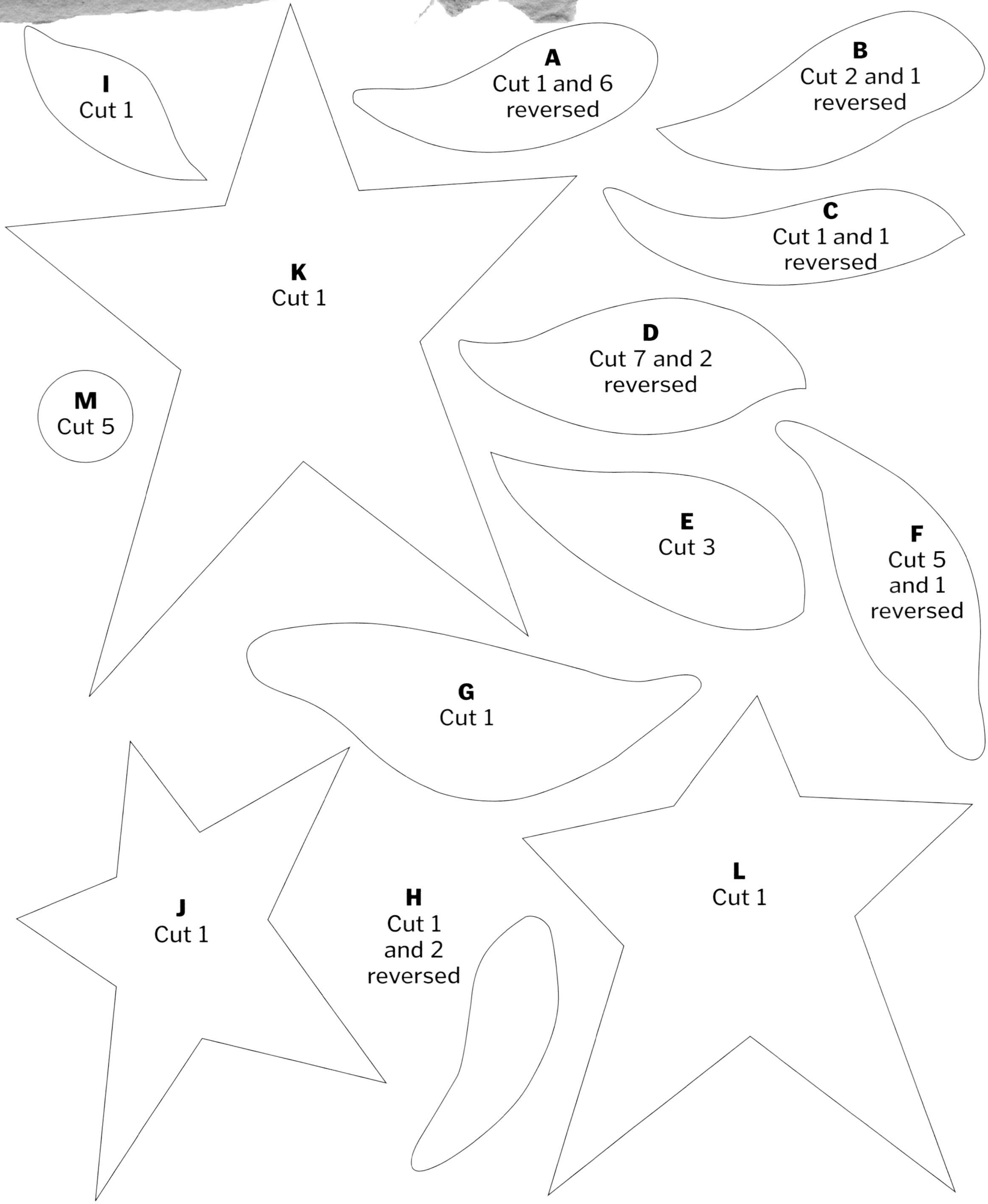

I
Cut 1

A
Cut 1 and 6
reversed

B
Cut 2 and 1
reversed

C
Cut 1 and 1
reversed

K
Cut 1

D
Cut 7 and 2
reversed

M
Cut 5

E
Cut 3

F
Cut 5
and 1
reversed

G
Cut 1

L
Cut 1

J
Cut 1

H
Cut 1
and 2
reversed

PINK LINARIA

LAMB'S EAR

MIXED PRIMROSE

VIOLAS 'ETAIN'

PURPLE LINARIA

VIOLAS 'ETAIN'

LAMB'S EAR

DWARF TRAILING SNAPDRAGON

SCOTCH MOSS

MIXED PRIMROSE

DWARF TRAILING SNAPDRAGON

Summer Cottage

Summer Cottage

*T*he child in all of us is drawn to this tiny cottage garden! A miniature bench welcomes the flower fairies giving them a place to rest and keep a watchful eye on the bees buzzing around the bee skep. Grassy areas are created with thymus minus and wooly thyme. A pea gravel path leads the flower fairies to the cottage door. Inside you will find a hidden fairy message left behind on scraps of found tissue paper.

Small dwarf spruce and other dwarf conifers create a garden setting for our fairy cottage. Railroad enthusiasts have created a demand for dwarf shrubs, so many garden centers have these miniature conifers.

This fairy garden has been "planted" in a large iron garden urn. You could plant your cottage anywhere the flower fairies have been seen flitting about. Mix together one child, a garden chair, a fairy story and one cottage for a magical afternoon.

Position on a 20-inch square (Diagram is scaled down to 40% of original size. Enlarge pattern to 250%)

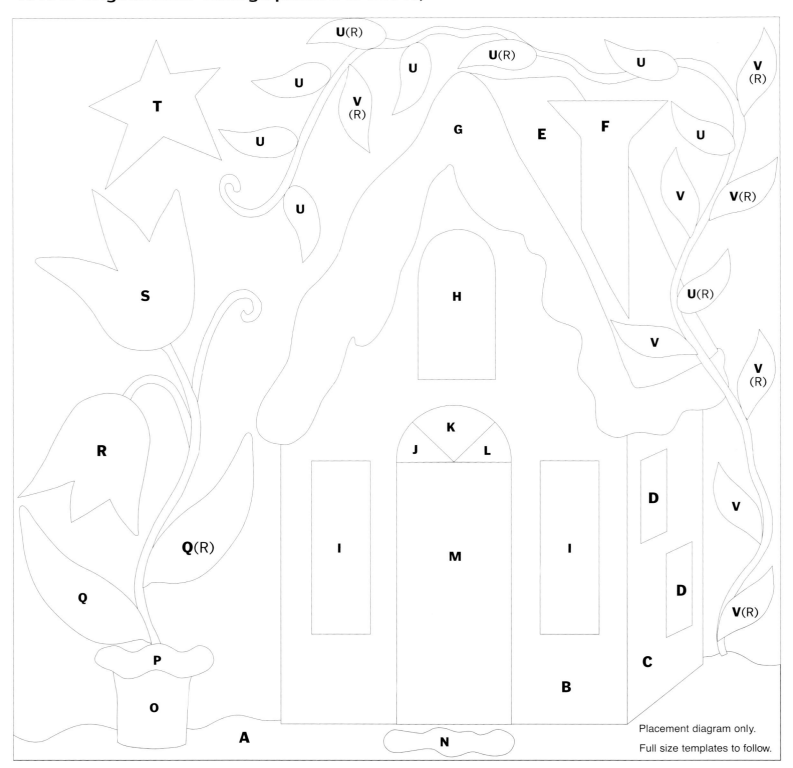

Placement diagram only.

Full size templates to follow.

Our appliquéd house is surrounded by summer vines and tulips.

BLOCK INSTRUCTIONS

- Cut the background block 20 1/2" x 20 1/2".

- Make 1/4" bias tape for flower and vine stems.

- Make the appliqué templates.

- Trace around the templates on the right side of your fabric for needle-turn appliqué. Refer to the picture to help with color choice.

- Cut out the shapes, adding your seam allowance.

- Follow the appliqué instructions on page 4 and sew the pieces to your background block.

SMALL DWARF CONIFER

THYMUS MINUS

WOOLY THYME

ITALIAN COTTAGE

SMALL DWARF SPRUCE

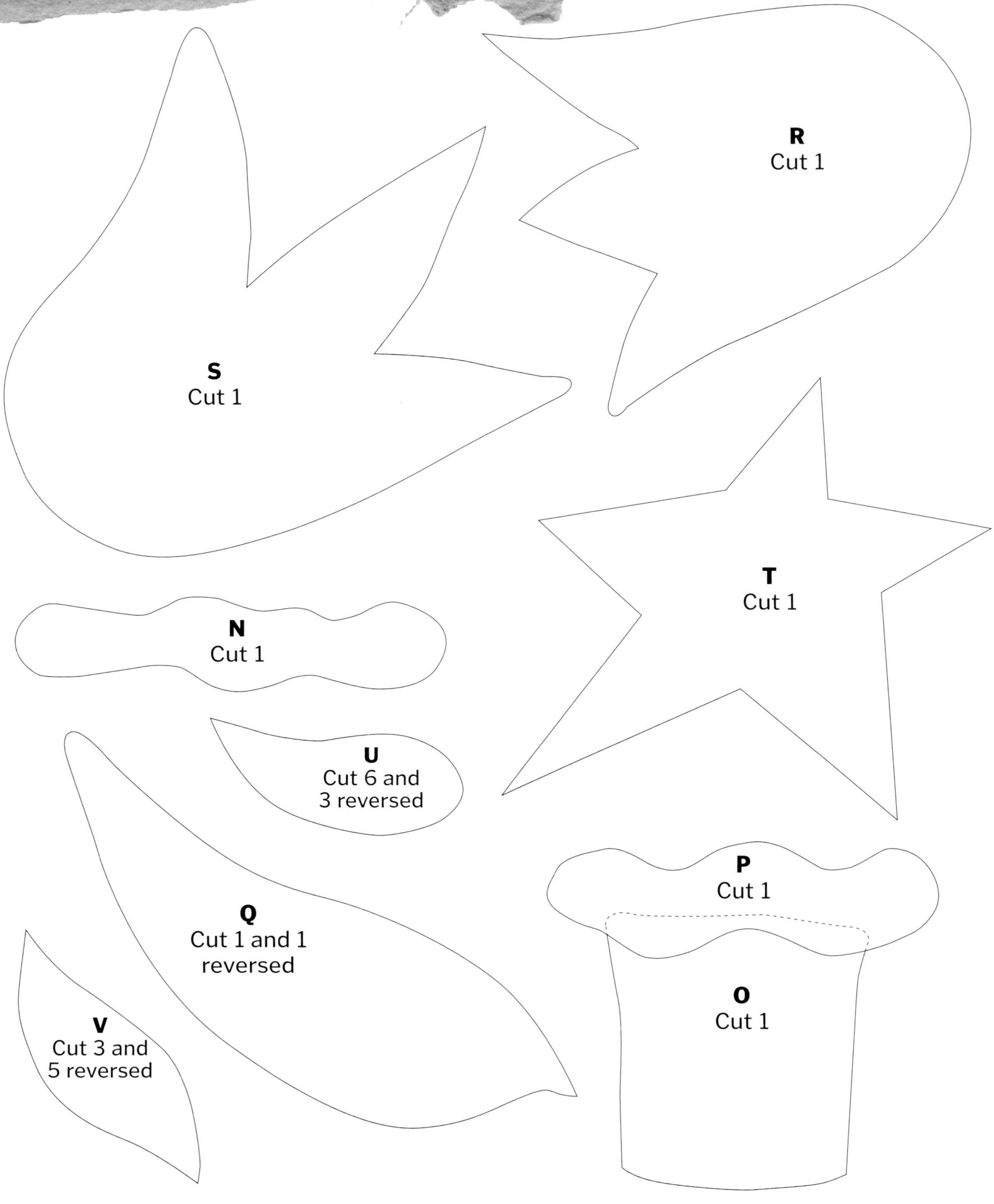

R
Cut 1

S
Cut 1

T
Cut 1

N
Cut 1

U
Cut 6 and
3 reversed

P
Cut 1

Q
Cut 1 and 1
reversed

V
Cut 3 and
5 reversed

O
Cut 1

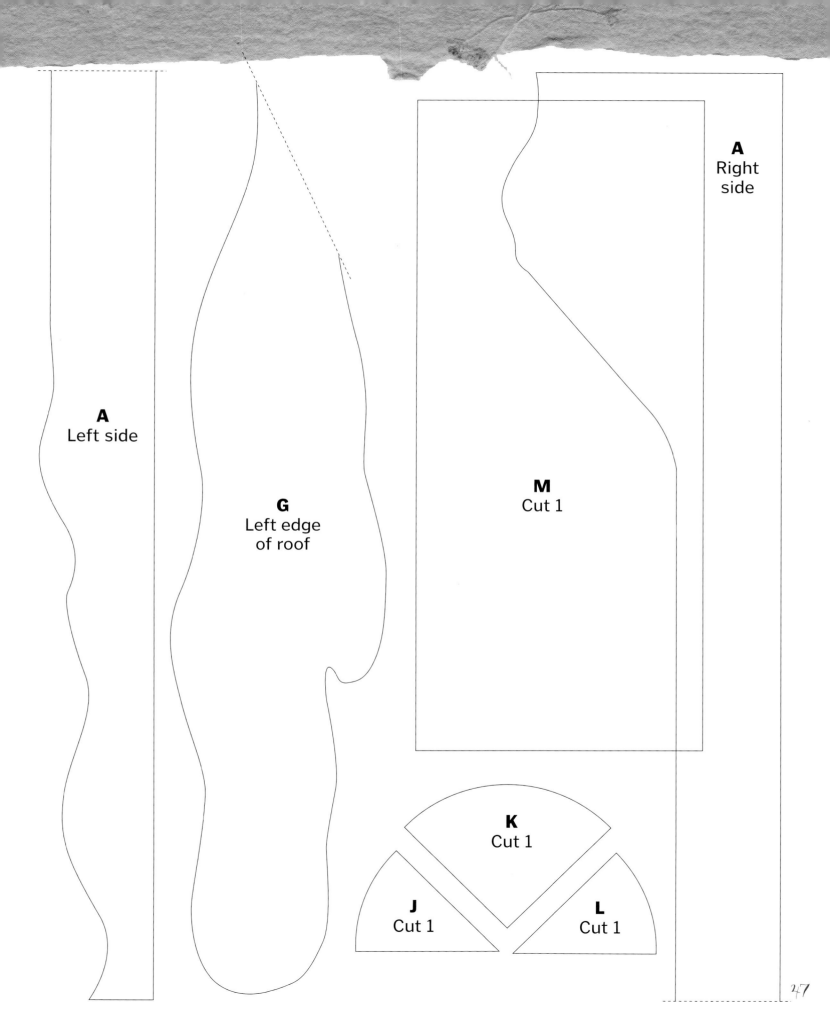

A
Left side

G
Left edge
of roof

M
Cut 1

A
Right
side

K
Cut 1

J
Cut 1

L
Cut 1

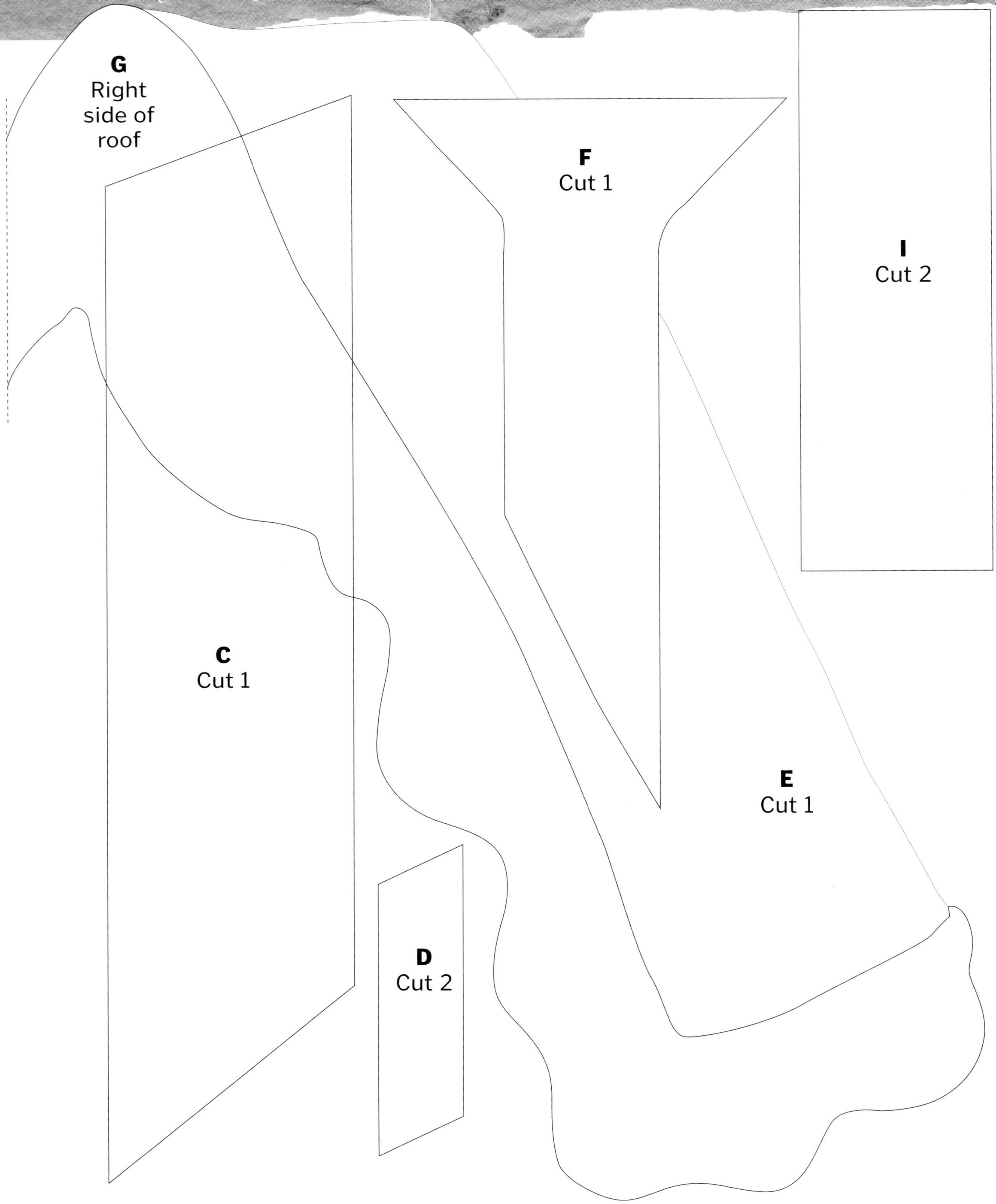

G
Right
side of
roof

F
Cut 1

I
Cut 2

C
Cut 1

E
Cut 1

D
Cut 2

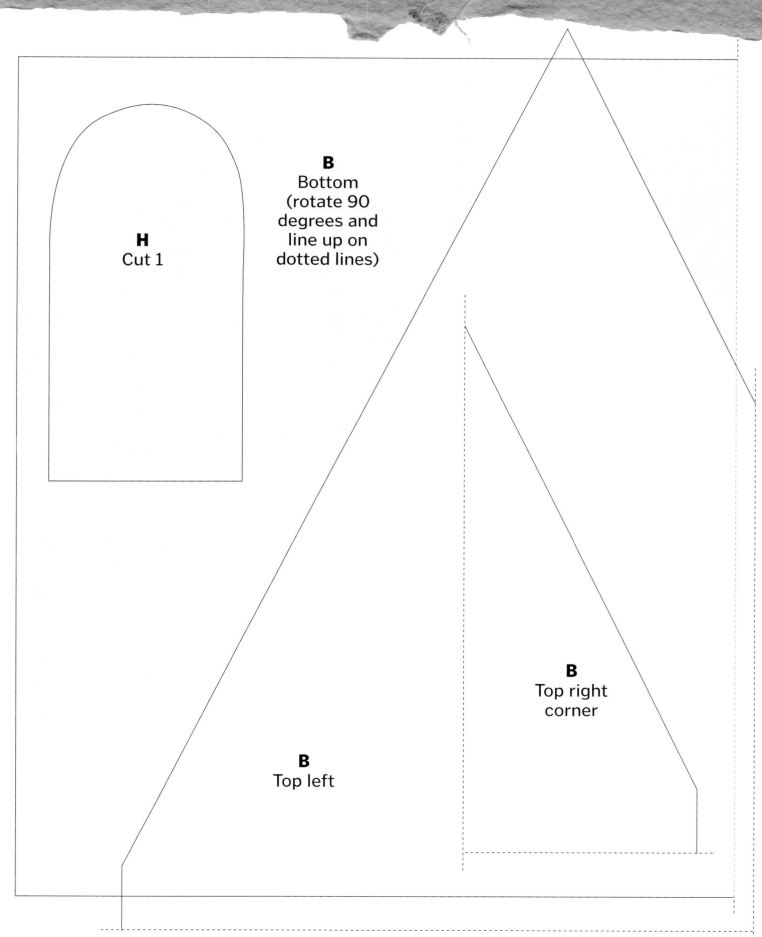

H
Cut 1

B
Bottom
(rotate 90
degrees and
line up on
dotted lines)

B
Top right
corner

B
Top left

49

Autumn's Hurrah

Autumn's Hurrah

*I*n Kansas, cool autumn evenings offer a respite from our humid August heat. Summer flowers seem to recover from the doldrums and are rejuvenated in their containers. They glow in the cooler temperatures.

Hummingbirds flit from flower to flower, drinking nectar, readying for their long migration south. Butterflies make their last visits to autumn flowers before finding a place to winter-over. We leave the air-conditioned refuge of our homes and approach the outside anew. Nature begins her spectacular show as the trees dress in their fall colors.

Summer pots may easily be transformed to capture the look of the autumn season. Remove spent plants and add small mums to your summer container gardens. Small mum plants may be purchased at any garden center and are the perfect size to tuck into your summer plantings.

This black iron urn contains 'Blackie' sweet-potato vine, 'Honeylove' lantana, coleus, spikes of red fountain grass, and whimsical swirls of annual eucalyptus. Lavender colored mums have been tucked into this planting to celebrate the up-coming fall season.

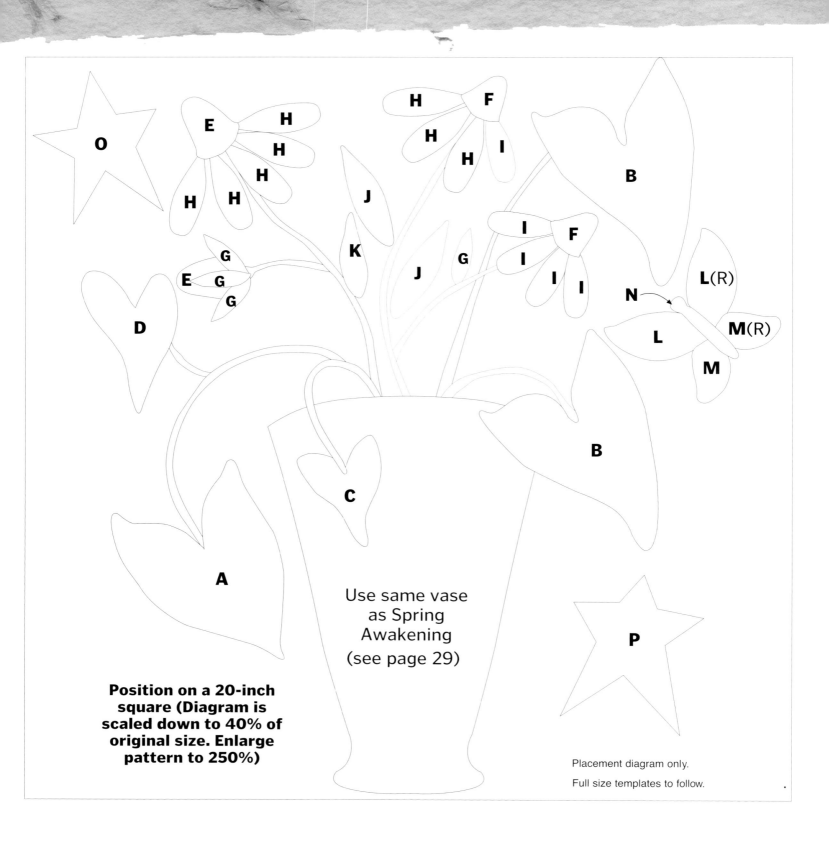

Use same vase
as Spring
Awakening
(see page 29)

Position on a 20-inch square (Diagram is scaled down to 40% of original size. Enlarge pattern to 250%)

Placement diagram only.

Full size templates to follow.

Cone flowers attract butterflies, native bees and goldfinch. Their orange and purple flowers are "abuzz" with insect activity all summer and fall. Their long season of bloom and drought resistance makes them the perfect garden flower. Leave the faded blooms in your garden all winter long. Goldfinch feed on their seeds during the winter when food is scarce.

BLOCK INSTRUCTIONS

- Cut the background block 20 1/2" x 20 1/2".

- Make 1/4" bias tape for flower and vine stems.

- Make the appliqué templates.

- Trace around the templates on the right side of your fabric for needle-turn appliqué. Refer to the picture to help with color choice.

- Cut out the shapes, adding your seam allowance.

- Follow the appliqué instructions on page 4 and sew the pieces to your background block.

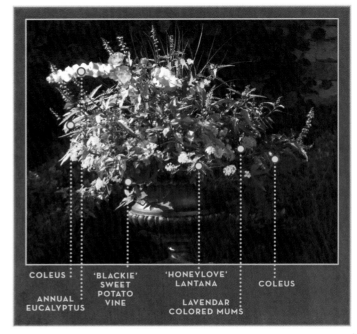

COLEUS 'BLACKIE' SWEET POTATO VINE 'HONEYLOVE' LANTANA COLEUS

ANNUAL EUCALYPTUS LAVENDAR COLORED MUMS

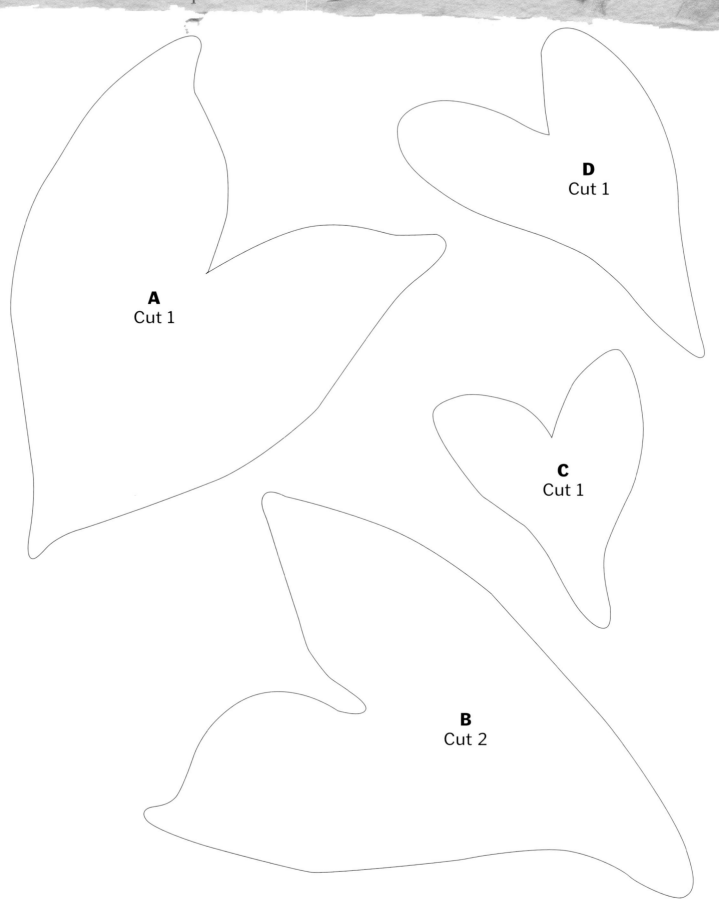

A
Cut 1

D
Cut 1

C
Cut 1

B
Cut 2

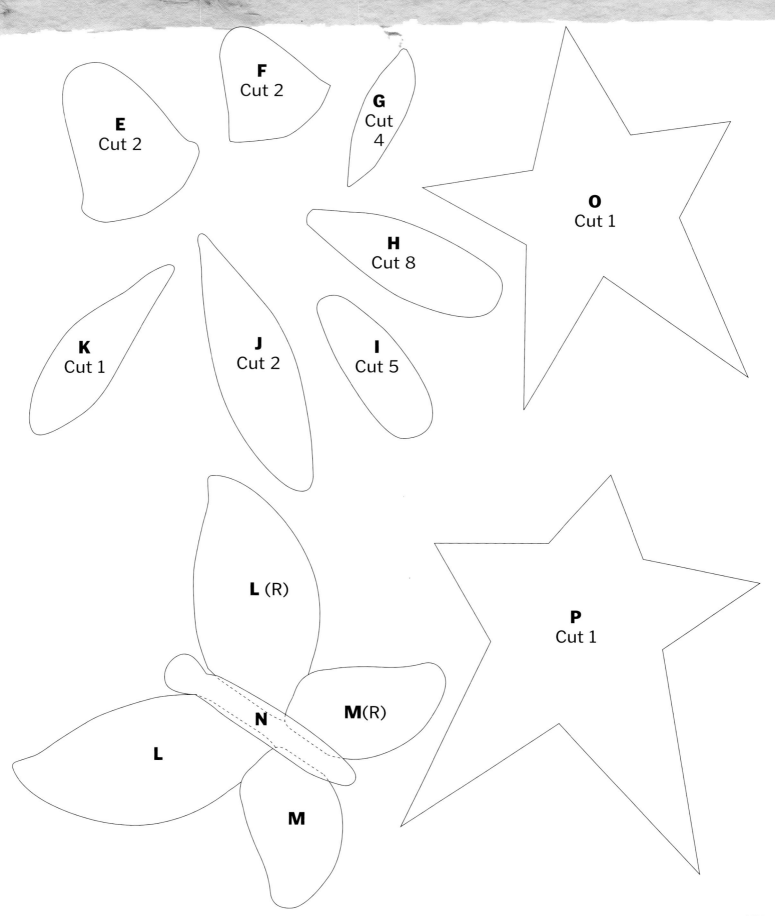

E
Cut 2

F
Cut 2

G
Cut 4

O
Cut 1

H
Cut 8

K
Cut 1

J
Cut 2

I
Cut 5

L (R)

P
Cut 1

N

L

M(R)

M

Autumn Splendor

Autumn Splendor

Ricki loves the look of grasses in fall plantings. The movement of grass and their seed heads as they dance in the wind is almost lyrical. The grasses bring harvest time to mind.

When choosing grasses for your container garden, look for the carex family of grasses. These perennial grasses are shorter and their brilliant foliage is the perfect addition to the garden and containers.

In this mossy terracotta container, 'Toffee Twist' carex grass adds a bronzed spiky architecture to the planting. Rudbeckia repeats the sunset colors of fall and the lime-green geranium leaf looks as if it has been brushed with copper.

Nestled into the pot are those wonderful chartreuse hedge apples. Their fresh green this time of the year adds a special touch of color and light to the fall container. Later, Ricki exchanges the hedge apples for pumpkins or gourds.

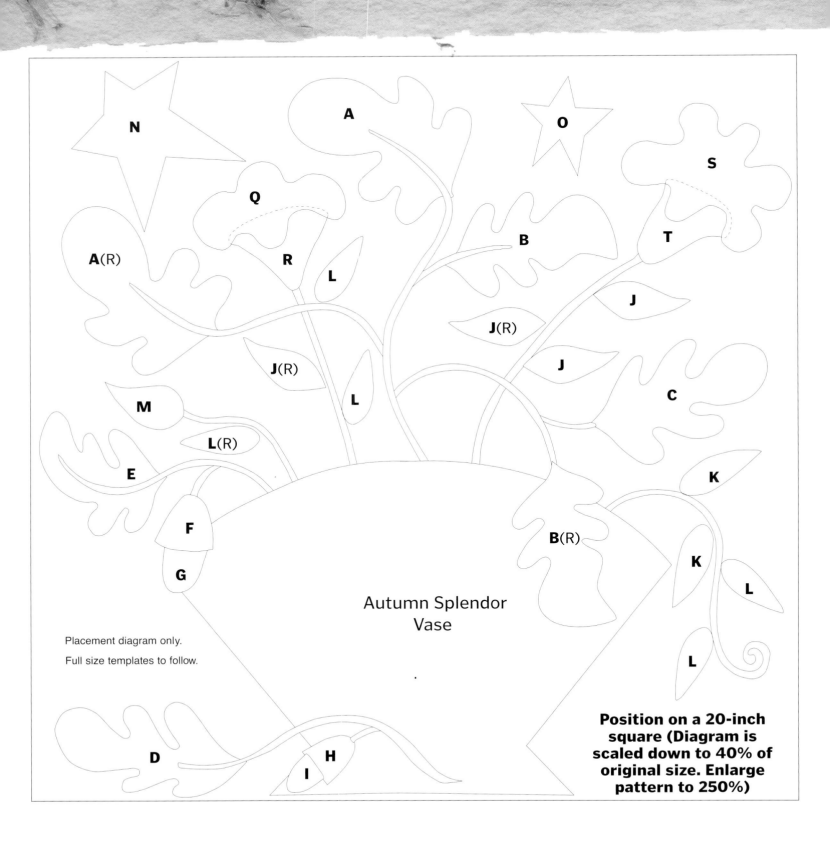

N

A

O

Q

S

A(R)

B

T

R

L

J

J(R)

J

J(R)

C

M

L(R)

E

K

L

F

B(R)

G

K

Autumn Splendor
Vase

L

Placement diagram only.

Full size templates to follow.

L

Position on a 20-inch square (Diagram is scaled down to 40% of original size. Enlarge pattern to 250%)

D

H

I

Oak leaves, acorns and cockscomb
fill our quilted autumn basket.

BLOCK INSTRUCTIONS

- ◾ Cut the background block 20 1/2" x 20 1/2".

- ◾ Make 1/4" bias tape for flower and vine stems.

- ◾ Make the appliqué templates.

- ◾ Trace around the templates on the right side of your fabric for needle-turn appliqué. Refer to the picture to help with color choice.

- ◾ Cut out the shapes, adding your seam allowance.

- ◾ Follow the appliqué instructions on page 4 and sew the pieces to your background block.

'VANCOUVER CENTENNIAL' GERANIUM

CAREX- 'TOFFEE TWIST' GRASS

'GRETCHEN' MUM

'GRETCHEN' MUM

'CHEROKEE SUNSET' RUDBECKIA

'SUNSPOT' HEUCHERELLA

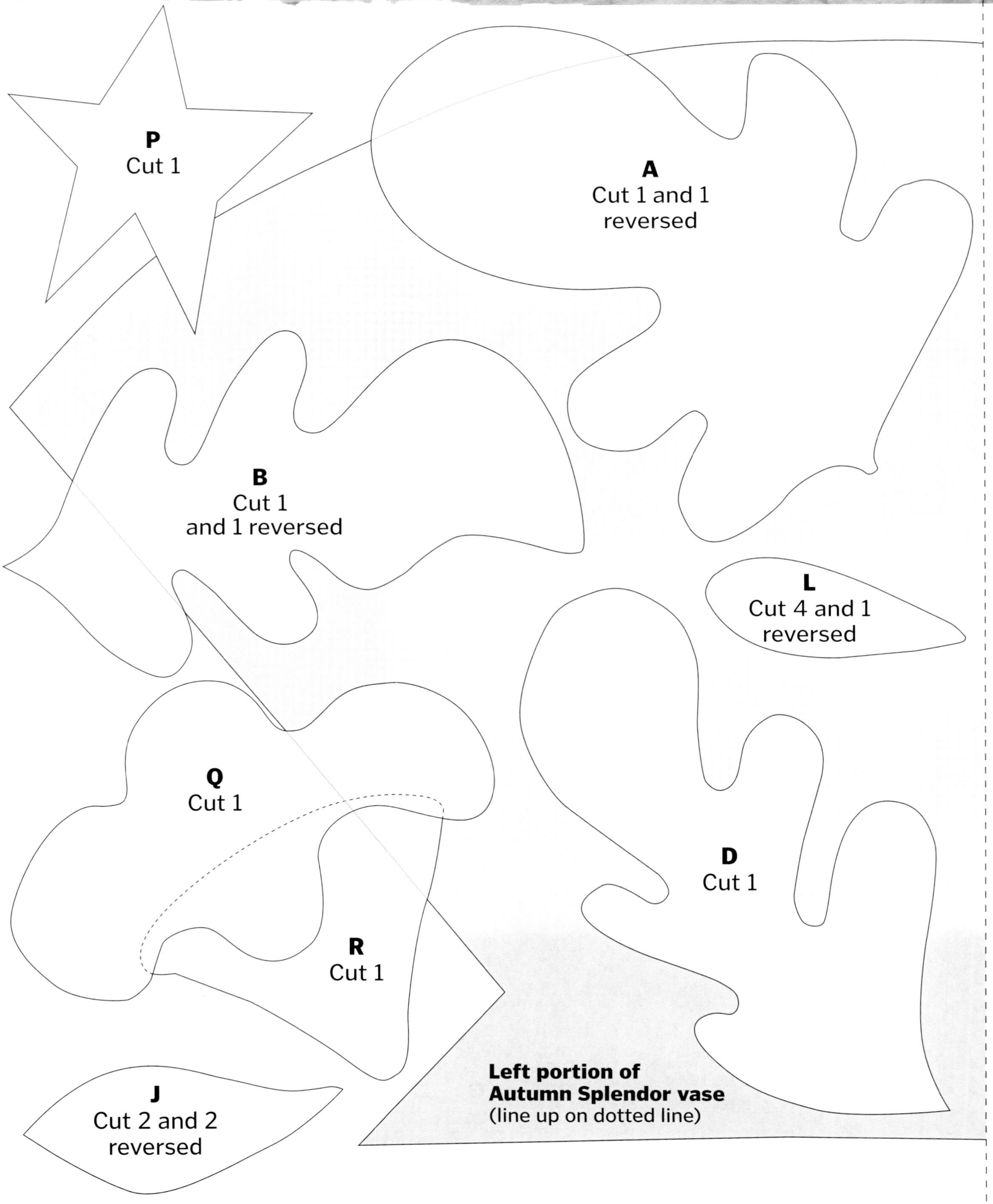

P
Cut 1

A
Cut 1 and 1
reversed

B
Cut 1
and 1 reversed

L
Cut 4 and 1
reversed

Q
Cut 1

D
Cut 1

R
Cut 1

J
Cut 2 and 2
reversed

**Left portion of
Autumn Splendor vase**
(line up on dotted line)

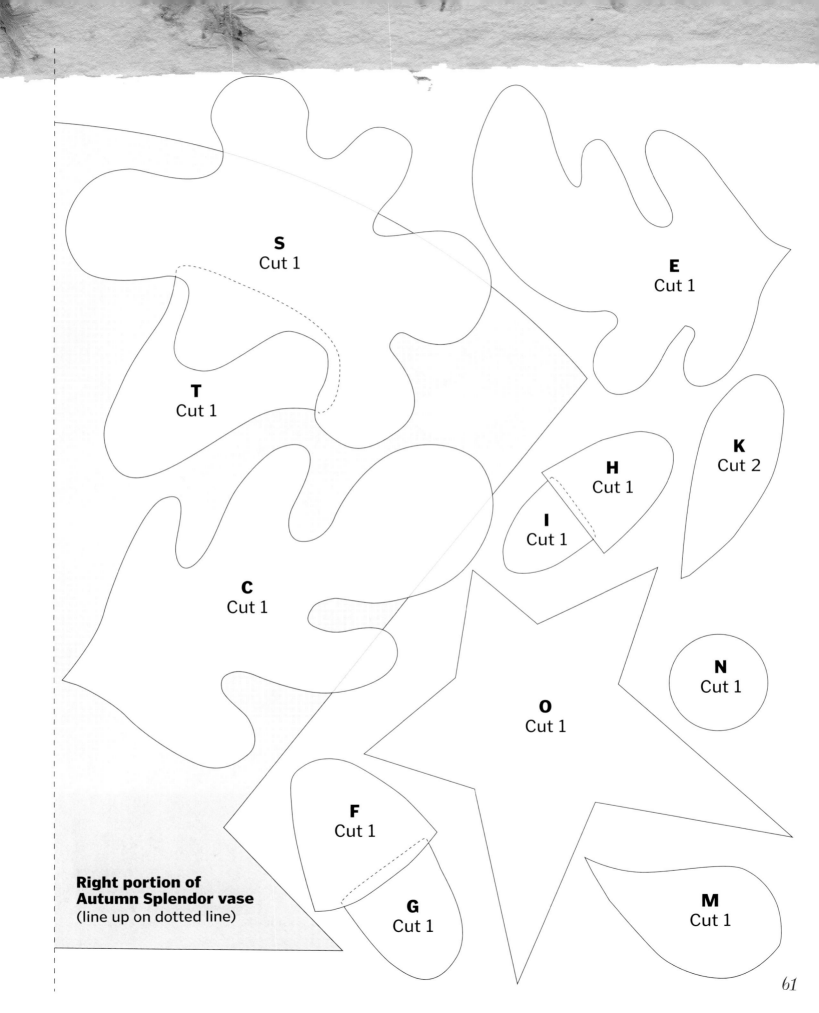

S
Cut 1

E
Cut 1

T
Cut 1

K
Cut 2

H
Cut 1

I
Cut 1

C
Cut 1

N
Cut 1

O
Cut 1

F
Cut 1

**Right portion of
Autumn Splendor vase**
(line up on dotted line)

G
Cut 1

M
Cut 1

BARB'S SUPPLY LIST

3 yds. red homespun for 2 block backgrounds, border, sashing blocks and binding

2 yds. red print for 3 block backgrounds, border and sashing blocks

1 1/2 yds each of 2 red prints for 4 block backgrounds and border blocks

1 yd. each of 2 medium tan prints

1 1/4 yd. of another medium tan print

3/4 yd. each of 3 green prints

Fat quarter of a light green print

1 yd. of light golden peach print

1 yd. peach print

3/4 yd. yellow print

1/2 yd. each of light gold print and homespun

1/2 yd. each of peach print and a check

1/4 yd. of plum print

Garden Glow

CHECK THE GALLERY AT THE BEGINNING OF THE BOOK! *Two different versions of the featured quilt are pictured. Barb and I began with the same nine block designs. The different sashing and border techniques lend a new look to each quilt. Pick your favorite border and sashing or design your own for a great finish!*

Barb's use of red background fabric heats up her garden! The pale peach, tan and gold prints are framed with the warm color of her background and the results are rich and inviting. The instructions for Barb's quilt follow on page 65.

Garden Glow

Appliqué by Leona Adams
Quilted by Jeanne Zyck

Garden Glow

Quilt size: 84" x 84"

BARB'S INSTRUCTIONS
All cutting measurements include
a 1/4" seam allowance.

▪ Appliqué the 9 featured blocks.

▪ Make a template for the sashing and border motif. Cut out 104 motifs from the assorted tan, peach and gold fabrics. Set aside 80 for the border.

▪ Cut 92 rectangles 4 1/2" x 8 1/2" from the assorted red fabrics. Set 68 aside for the border.

▪ Center the motif on the rectangle. The pointed tip of the motif should just touch the 1/4" seam allowance line. Appliqué in place. Repeat to complete 24 rectangles.

▪ Cut 16 squares 4 1/2" x 4 1/2" and set aside.

▪ Cut 4 squares 3 3/8" x 3 3/8" and turn them on point and appliqué them to four of the 4 1/2" squares. These will be used as cornerstone blocks between the rows of sashing strips.

▪ Refer to the diagram on the next page and sew the quilt top together.

Border Instructions

▪ Cut 4 squares 8 1/2" x 8 1/2" for the corner blocks from the assorted red fabrics. Refer to the picture of the quilt and appliqué three motifs to each square. Notice the center motif is aligned above the outside two motifs.

▪ Appliqué the motifs to the rectangles following the same method used for the sashing rectangles.

▪ Sew 4 strips each of 17 rectangles. Sew one strip to each side of the quilt top.

▪ Sew a corner square on both ends of the two remaining strips. Sew one strip each to the top and bottom of the quilt top.

Garden Glow

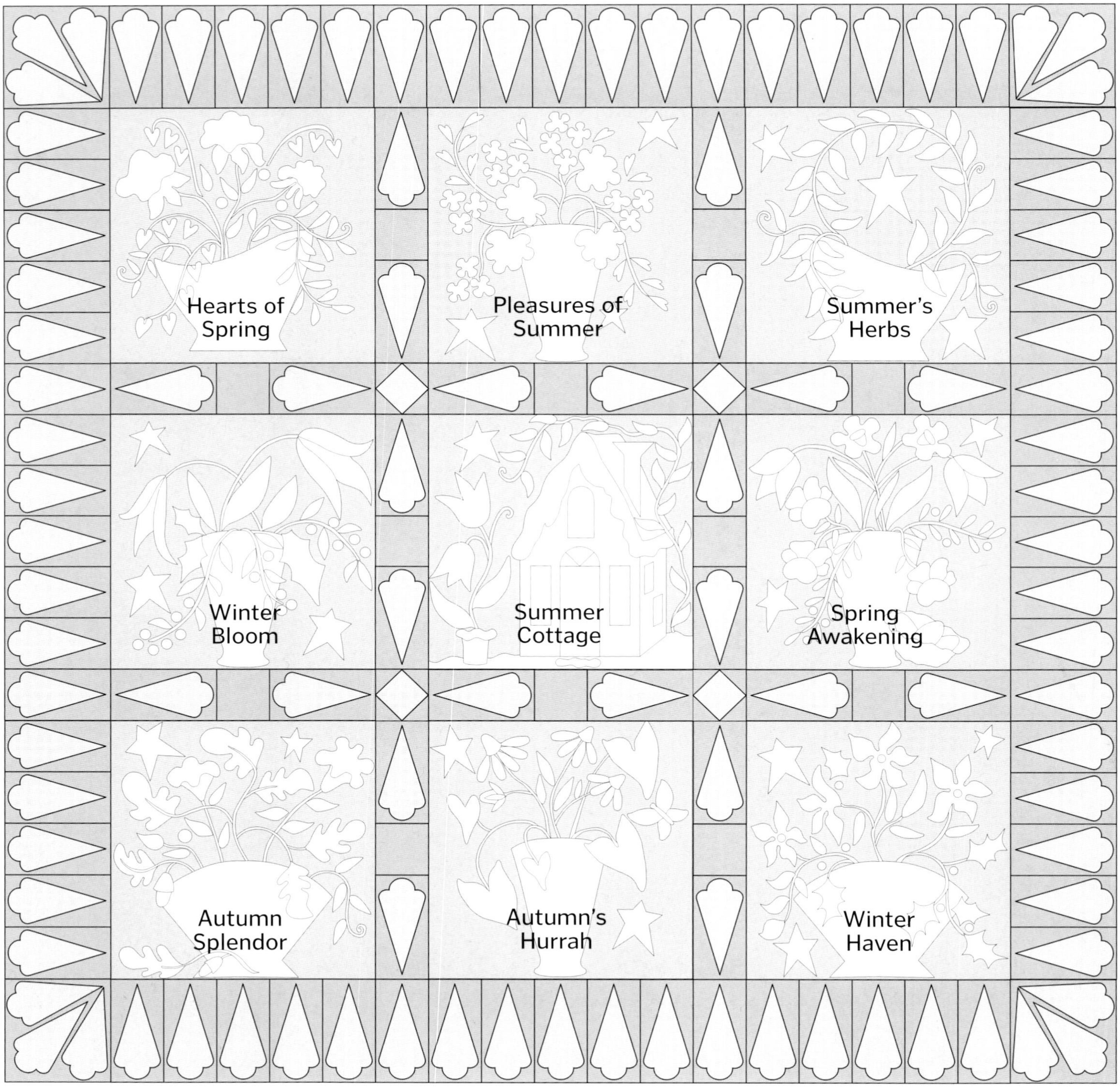

Hearts of
Spring

Pleasures of
Summer

Summer's
Herbs

Winter
Bloom

Summer
Cottage

Spring
Awakening

Autumn
Splendor

Autumn's
Hurrah

Winter
Haven

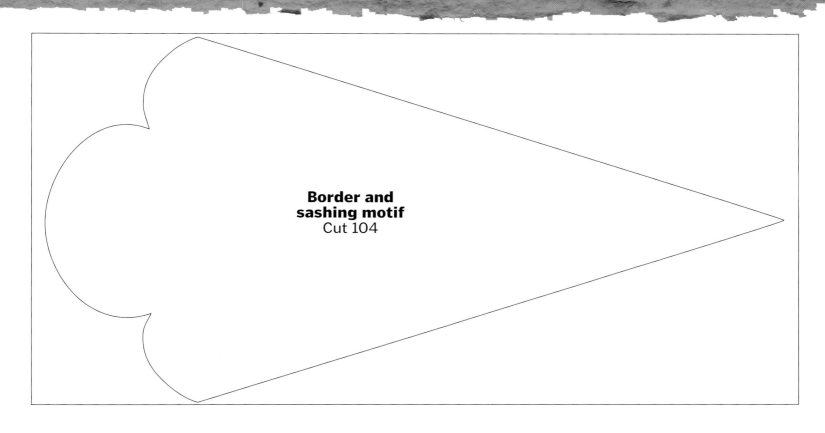

Border and sashing motif
Cut 104

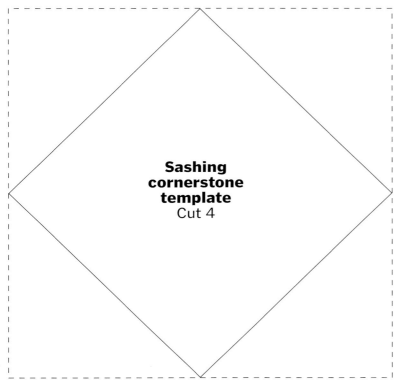

Sashing cornerstone template
Cut 4

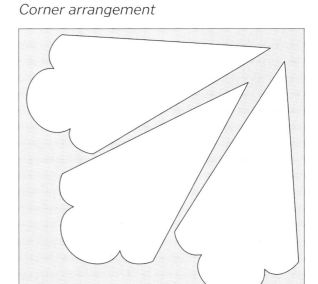

Corner arrangement

Garden glow border pieces

Cottage Garden

Appliqué by Jean Stanclift
Quilted by Jeanne Zyck

ALMA'S SUPPLY LIST

5/8 yd. each of 3 light green background prints

1 1/4 yd. of another light green background print

3/4 yd. each of 2 red prints for flowers and half-square triangle units

3 yds. red print for border, flowers and half-square triangle units

1/3 yd. each of 3 pink print for berries and half-square triangle units

Scraps of yellow prints for stars and flowers

1/2 yd. each of 3 eggplant prints

1 fat quarter of another eggplant print

Fat quarter of black large scale floral for peaked pattern of roof

Scraps of black prints for roof and chimney

Scraps of brown tones for nest, butterfly & acorns

Scraps of cream shades for the eggs & windows

1/2 yd. each of 6 green prints, for leaves, bias vines & half-square triangles

Fat quarters of 3 green prints half-square triangles

3/4 yd. green stripe for binding

2" finished half-square triangle paper

CHECK THE GALLERY AT THE BEGINNING OF THE BOOK! Two different versions of the featured quilt are pictured. Barb and I began with the same nine block designs. The different sashing and border techniques lend a new look to each quilt. Pick your favorite border and sashing or design your own for a great finish.

Jeanne Zyck is responsible for the scalloped border treatment on my quilt. She thought scallops would be the perfect finish. I went home and couldn't stop thinking about the idea. I was shocked I had never thought of doing a scalloped border. After 30 years of quilting, and all of the fabric borders I have done, the idea never crossed my mind. I immediately asked my husband Dave to draft the scallops. The soft curve of the scallop is the perfect frame for this quilt. Thank you Jeanne and Dave.

Cottage Garden

Quilt size: 84" x 84"

ALMA'S INSTRUCTIONS
All cutting measurements include
a 1/4" seam allowance.

■ Appliqué the 9 featured blocks.

■ Use your favorite method for making 2" finished half-square triangles. I like to use the half-square triangle paper. The results are accurate with little fabric waste. Make 256 units.

Cottage Garden

- Sew 6 strips of 10 units each.

- Sew 4 strips of 32 units each.

- Sew 2 strips of 34 units each.

- Refer to the diagram of the quilt and sew the quilt top together.

Border Instructions

- Cut 2 strips 8 1/2" x 68 1/2" from the red print fabric. Sew one to each side of the quilt top.

- Cut 2 strips 8 1/2" x 84 1/2" from the red print fabric. Sew one each to the top and bottom of the quilt top.

- Use freezer paper to make the scallop template. Cut a piece 84" long. Trace the scallop template on the freezer paper. Align and continue to trace until you have a corner scallop and 5 side scallops. End the strip with another corner scallop. Set the template aside.

- Quilt the top before cutting the scallops. The quilting design keeps the fabric border from stretching after the the scallops are cut. The scallop border design is drafted for an 84" long border. The quilting takes up the fabric and reduces the length of the border. To adjust for the change in size of your quilted border, make small folds in the paper template along the flat, inside curve to reduce its length. These small adjustments in the template are not noticeable in the finished quilt.

84 1/2" x 8 1/2"

12"

8 1/2" x 64 1/2"

Hearts of Spring

Pleasures of Summer

Summer's Herbs

Spring Awakening

Summer Cottage

Winter Bloom

8 1/2" x 64 1/2"

Autumn Splendor

Autumn's Hurrah

Winter Haven

84 1/2" x 8 1/2"

C   B   A

D

Scalloped pattern shape on following pages

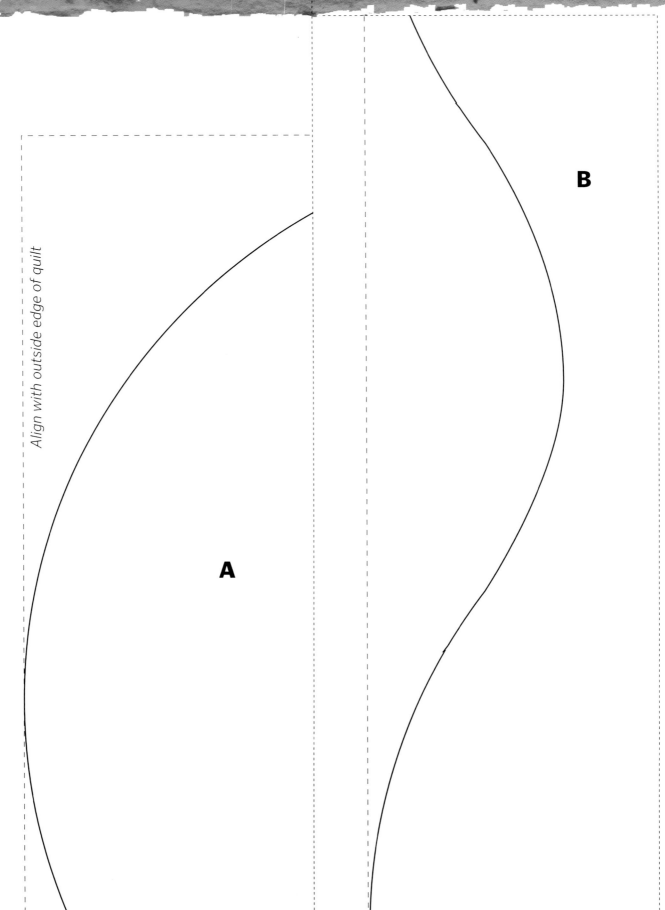

Align with outside edge of quilt

A

B

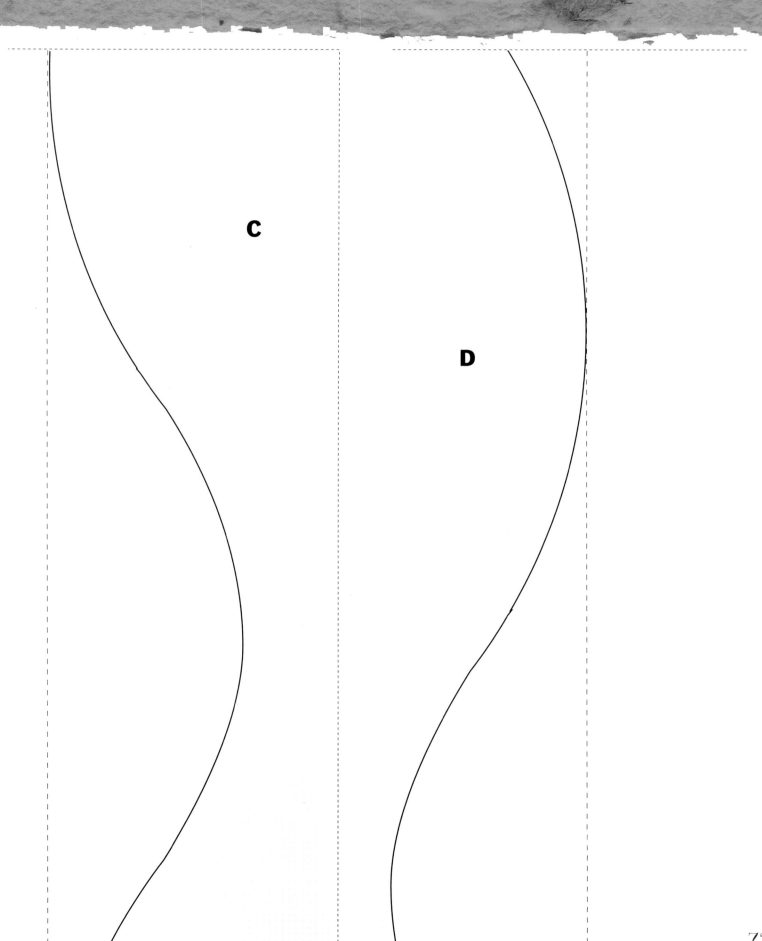

C

D

73

Garden Glow Sheet set & Pillow shams

SUPPLY LIST

- 1 Sheet Set
- 1 1/4 yd. light fabric to match sheet set
- 1 lace placemat for each pillow sham
- 1/2 yd. fabric for each pillow sham
- 1 bag poly-fil for each pillow sham

SHEET INSTRUCTIONS
All cutting measurements include
a 1/4" seam allowance.

- Cut 3" wide bias strips from the light fabric and sew them together for the sheet ruffle. You will need about 215" of length for the ruffle.

- Roll-hem both sides and ends of the strip.

- Sew a gathering stitch along the center of the ruffle. Gather the ruffle to fit the sheet heading. Center the wrong side of the ruffle on top of the right side of the sheet heading. Pin the ruffle in place along the seam line. While pinning, ease the gathered ruffle evenly across the sheet heading.

- Sew along the center of the ruffle attaching it to the sheet heading. Remove the gathering stitch and press.

PILLOWCASE INSTRUCTIONS

- Cut 3" wide bias strips from the light fabric and sew them together for the pillowcase ruffle. You will need about 120" of length for each pillowcase.

- Roll-hem both sides of the strip.

- Sew a gathering stitch along the center of the ruffle. Gather the ruffle to fit the pillowcase heading.

- Place the ends of the ruffle, right sides together, and stitch.

- Center the wrong side of the ruffle, on top of the right side of the pillowcase heading. Pin the ruffle in place along the seam line. While pinning, ease the gathered ruffle evenly across the pillowcase heading.

- Sew along the center of the ruffle attaching it to the pillowcase heading. Remove the gathering stitch and press.

PILLOW SHAM INSTRUCTIONS
All cutting measurements include a
1/2" seam allowance.

- Measure your placemats. Add 2 1/2" to the length and width. Use this measurement to cut out the pillow top and back.

- With right sides together, stitch the pillow top to the pillow backing. Use 1/2" seam allowance. Leave a 5" opening along one side to stuff.

- Turn pillow to the right side and press. Top stitch 1/4" from the seam line along all sides. Do not stitch over the opening.

- Center the placemats on the pillow top and whip stitch in place.

- Fill with poly-fil and blind stitch the opening

Cottage Garden Top Sheet & Pillow

SHEET INSTRUCTIONS

All cutting measurements include a
1/4" seam allowance.

- Cut 2 lengths of the light colored fabric each 45" x 76".

- Sew the two, right sides together, along the long edge with a 1/2" seam allowance. Fold the raw edge of the seam allowance to the inside and top stitch to finish.

- Roll-hem both sides and the bottom of the sheet.

- Cut 3" wide bias strips from the light fabric and sew them together for the ruffle. You will need about 215" of length for the ruffle.

- Fold the ruffle in half lengthwise, wrong sides together and press.

- Gather the ruffle. With right sides together, pin the ruffle to the sheet top. While pinning, ease the gathered ruffle evenly along the edge.

- Sew the ruffle to the sheet top.

- Cut 3" wide bias strips from the light fabric and sew them together for the facing. You will need 75" of length for the facing.

- Sew the facing to the sheet top, right sides together.

- Fold the heading to the back of the sheet and press.

- Roll-hem the facing and stitch in place.

PILLOWCASE INSTRUCTIONS:

- Cut a length of fabric 45" x 60".

- Refold the fabric right sides together.

- Sew the end of the pillowcase closed.

- Sew the side seam closed.

- Fold a 6" heading to the inside and turn under a 3" hem. Stitch a straight stitch with the machine to finish.

- Turn the pillowcase to the right side and press.

- Evenly space three buttonholes on the top heading of the pillowcase.

- Align and stitch three buttons to the inside of the heading, directly opposite the three buttonhole openings.

- Slip the body pillow into the pillowcase and button to finish.

Design by Barb Adams
Sewing by Leona Adams

Seasonal Purses

SUPPLY LIST

To purchase pre-made purses ready to embellish:
- ■ Purses from Moda fabrics
  Red- Stock #995-28
  Black- Stock #995-29
  Tan- Stock #995-30

To sew your own:
- ■ 2/3 yd. prairie cloth or wool (54" wide)
- ■ 1/3 yd. lining
- ■ 1 yd. iron-on interfacing
- ■ button
- ■ Scraps of wool

PURSE INSTRUCTIONS
*Cutting measurements include
a 1/2" seam allowance.*

- ■ Cut one strip of fabric 9" x 19" for the purse body.

- ■ Cut 2 flaps 8 1/2" x 10".

- ■ Cut one button loop 1 1/2" x 3"

- ■ Cut the lining 9" x 18 1/2".

- ■ Cut the strap 2" x 54".

- ■ Cut one piece of iron-on interfacing 8 1/2" x 10". Cut another piece 9" x 19". Set aside.

- ■ Fold the strap in half lengthwise and turn the seam allowance to the inside. Top stitch closed. Adjust the strap to a comfortable purse length and trim. Set aside.

The pre-made purses can be purchased from your local quilt shop. They are ready for embellishment. The purse pattern is provided if you would rather make your own. Grab scraps of wool and make a purse for Summer, Fall and Winter. Add beads that match your wool for an extra sparkle.

- ■ Fold the button loop in half lengthwise and turn the seam allowance to the inside. Top stitch closed. Set aside.

- ■ Iron interfacing to the wrong side of the fabric of the purse and one side of the flap.

- ■ Fold the purse fabric in half, right sides together, to form a rectangle 9" x 9 1/2". Stitch both side seams together.

- ■ Center the button loop on the the right side of one flap as illustrated. Tack into place.

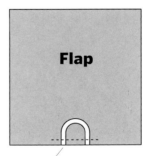

Flap

Loop sewn in place

- ■ Place the right sides of the flap together. Sew three sides together. Turn to the right side and press.

Seasonal Purses

Slip the flap inside the purse. Pin the back of the flap to the purse back. Position the strap inside the purse. Pin the one end of the strap to each side of the flap. Pin into place.

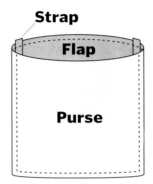

Sew across the seam line to attach the flap and strap to the purse and set aside.

Fold the purse lining in half, right sides together, to form a rectangle 9" x 9 1/4". Stitch both side seams together. Leave a 4" opening on one of the sides.

Turn the lining to the right side and slip it into the purse and sew all around the top to close.

Sew lining inside purse

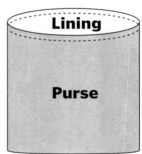

Pull the lining out of the purse and turn the purse to the right side through the opening of the lining.

Whip stitch the opening closed and slip the lining back into the purse. Mold the purse into shape.

Align the button with the button loop and sew into place.

APPLIQUÉ INSTRUCTIONS

Use freezer paper to make templates of the appliqué shapes.

Iron the slick side of the paper to the right side of the wool.

Cut the wool shapes out. Do not add a seam allowance.

Place the shapes on your background. Refer to the picture for placement.

Baste shapes into place with tacky glue.

Use one strand of matching floss or thread to appliqué the shapes to the background wool. Whip-stitch the shapes in place.

Summer purse: Stem stitch the vine with three strands of green floss.

STEM STITCH DETAIL

Add beads along the leaf veins and flower centers.

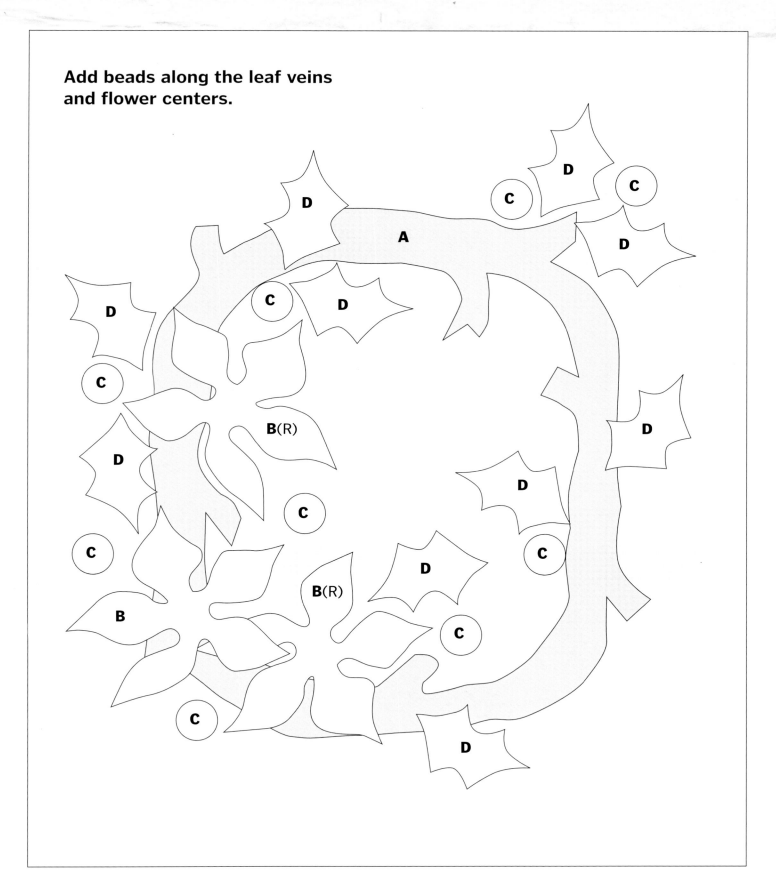

Spring's Arrival

Quilt size: 29 1/2" x 29 1/2"

SUPPLY LIST

- Fat quarter each of 4 pink fabrics
- Fat quarter each of 3 green fabrics
- 1 1/4 yd. large scale pink floral for quilt blocks, backing and binding
- DMC floss #223 (pink) 5 skeins
- DMC floss #3012 (green) 5 skeins
- Embroidery needle

Design by Alma Allen
Embroidery design by Sherry Carey
Piecing and Appliqué by Jean Stanclift
Quilting by Leona Adams

Embroidery stitches add whimsey and texture to this wall-sized quilt. Instead of using the typical quilt stitch, Sherry Carey outlined and filled these tulip and star shapes with the button-hole, lazy daisy and herringbone stitches. Sherry's stitches are done through all three layers of the quilt and offer added design and texture on the front and back of the quilt. This look is an updated version of the Victorian Crazy Quilt embellishment. We asked Sherry to do four of these blocks to give you an idea of how the entire surface could be quilted.

Spring's Arrival

INSTRUCTIONS FOR PIECED STAR BLOCK:

- Make templates from freezer paper. You will need one template for each piece. Make a reverse template for A, D and E. Each template is made the exact size of the pattern piece without the seam allowance.

- Iron the freezer paper template, with the shiny side down, to the wrong side of your fabric. Leave enough room between pieces to add your seam allowance.

- Cut out each piece, adding your 1/4" seam allowance. Using a plastic ruler and rotary cutter will make your seam allowances accurate.

- Pin the pieces together at the points of the freezer paper top and bottom and line up the edges of the fabric.

- Using the freezer paper as the seam guide, sew the pieces together. Refer to the block sewing guide.

- Carefully peel the freezer paper templates away from the wrong side of the fabric after the block is sewn. The freezer paper templates may be used more than one time if they are not torn.

- Piece 13 star blocks. Refer to the picture for color placement.

INSTRUCTIONS FOR APPLIQUÉ TULIP BLOCK:

- Cut 3 background blocks 6 1/2" x 6 1/2".

- Make templates of the appliqué shapes with template plastic. Do not add the seam allowance to these plastic shapes.

- Trace around the shape for needle-turn appliqué with a marking pencil that will show up on your fabric. The drawn line indicates your seam line.

- Cut out the fabric shapes, adding your seam allowance.

- Fold the background fabric in half vertically and horizontally. Finger-press the folds. Open the fabric.

- Center the design on the background block using the fold lines as a guide. Refer to the picture for placement.

- Baste the shapes into place on the background block.

- Appliqué the shapes to the background block.

- Refer to the picture and sew the quilt top together.

86

FIRST BORDER:

- Cut 2 border strips 1 1/4" x 24 1/2". Sew one strip to each side of the quilt top.

- Cut 2 border strips 1 1/4" x 26". Sew one strip to the top and one to the bottom of the quilt top.

SECOND BORDER:

- Cut 4 border strips 2 1/2" x 26". Sew one strip to each side of the quilt top.

- Cut 4 squares 2 1/2" x 2 1/2" from the dark rose print.

- Sew one 2 1/2" dark, rose-print square to each end of the two remaining border strips. Sew one border strip to the top and one to the bottom of the quilt top.

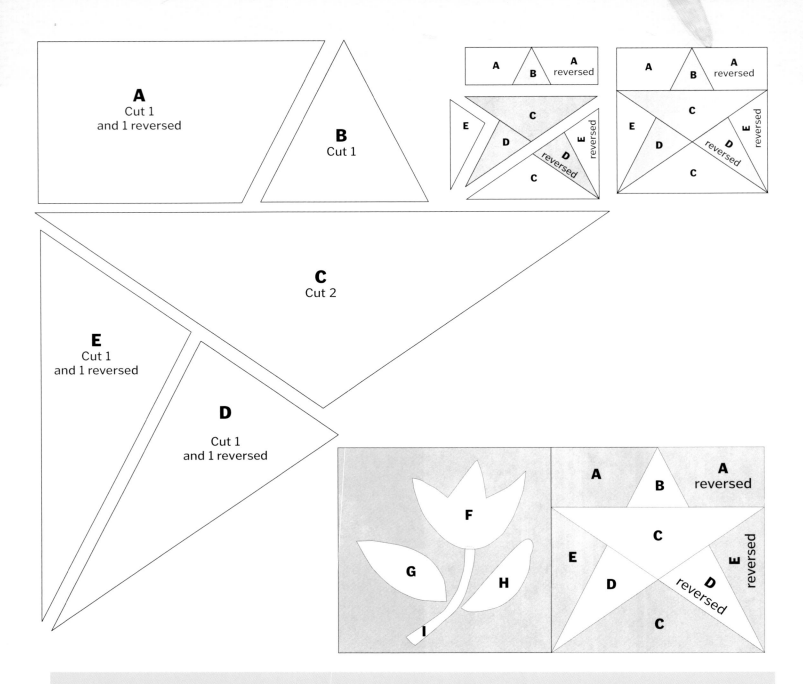

STAR BLOCKS:
TEMPLATES AND INSTRUCTIONS

These stars can be pieced accurately! Using a freezer paper template for a seam guide can make this process much easier. Trace each pattern piece of the star to the dull side of the freezer paper with a fine-tipped pen or sharp pencil.

It is possible to cut out several copies of a template at once. Trace the templates to one piece of freezer paper. Place the traced template sheet on top of several more pieces of freezer paper. Gently tack the freezer paper sheets together with the tip of a hot iron for several seconds. This keeps the paper from slipping when you cut out more than one template at a time. After cutting out the templates, carefully separate and label them.

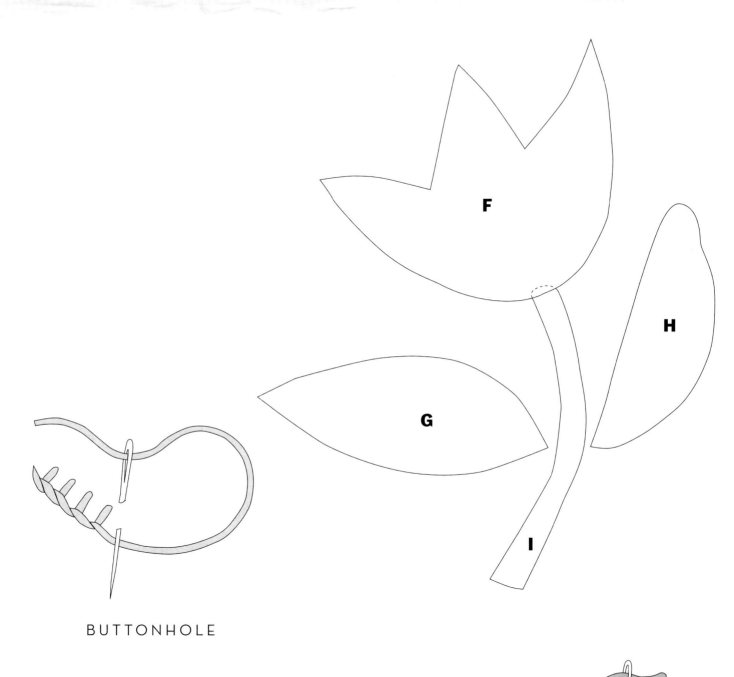

BUTTONHOLE

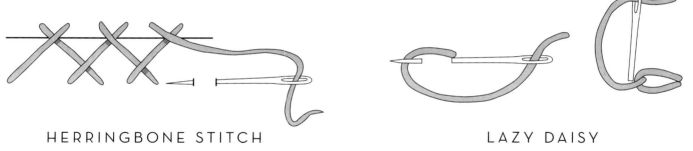

HERRINGBONE STITCH

LAZY DAISY

In Bloom

In Bloom

Design by Alma Allen
Piecing by Lynne Droege
Quilting design by Jeanne Zyck

Quilt size: 68" x 85"

SUPPLY LIST:

- Fat quarter each of 9 pink fabrics
- Fat quarter each of 10 green fabrics
- Fat quarter each of 9 light fabrics
- 1 1/2 yd. large scale light floral for setting squares and triangles
- 1/2 yd. burgundy check for the first border (1 1/2" wide strips are pieced for border length)
- 3/4 yd. green and pink ticking stripe (3" wide strips are pieced for border length)
- 1 1/3 yd. burgundy floral (5 1/2" wide strips are pieced for border length)

The use of the large scale floral print for the alternating blocks adds movement to the quilt top. To "tame" it down a bit, I used consistent placement of color. The result is a tropical paradise perfect for a room that needs a punch of color and bloom!

FOR EACH BLOCK:

All cutting measurements include 1/4" seam allowance.

- Cut 1 square 4 1/2" x 4 1/2" from the pink fabric for piece A.

- Cut 2 burgundy, 1 light and 1 green square 5 1/4" x 5 1/4". Cut each in half on the diagonal twice for piece B.

- Cut 8 pink squares 2 1/2" x 2 1/2" for piece C.

- Cut 4 light squares 2 7/8" x 2 7/8". Cut in half on the diagonal once for piece D.

- Cut 4 burgundy squares 2 7/8" x 2 7/8". Cut in half once on the diagonal for piece D.

- Refer to the piecing diagram and piece one block.

- Repeat the above for 11 more blocks.

SEWING THE QUILT TOP TOGETHER:

■ Cut 6 squares 12 1/2" x 12 1/2" from the large scale floral. Set these squares aside.

■ Cut 2 squares 18 1/4" x 18 1/4". Cut each square in half twice on the diagonal. Use one of these triangles as a template and cut two more. Make sure the base of the next two triangles is on the grain of the fabric. Set these triangles aside.

■ Cut 2 squares 9 3/8" x 9 3/8". Cut each square in half on the diagonal once. These triangles will be the corner triangles. Set them aside.

■ Refer to the quilt diagram and sew the quilt top together.

FIRST BORDER: BURGUNDY CHECK

■ Cut 2 strips 1 1/2" x 68 1/2". Sew one to each side of the quilt top.

■ Cut 2 strips 1 1/2" x 53 1/2". Sew one to the top and one to the bottom of the quilt top.

SECOND BORDER: TICKING STRIPE

■ Cut 2 strips 3" x 70 1/2". Sew one to each side of the quilt top.

■ Cut 2 strips 3" x 58 1/2". Sew one to the top and one to the bottom of the quilt top.

THIRD BORDER: BURGUNDY FLORAL

■ Cut 2 strips 5 1/2" x 75 1/2". Sew one to each side of the quilt top.

■ Cut 2 strips 5 1/2" x 68 1/2 ". Sew one to the top and one to the bottom of the quilt top.

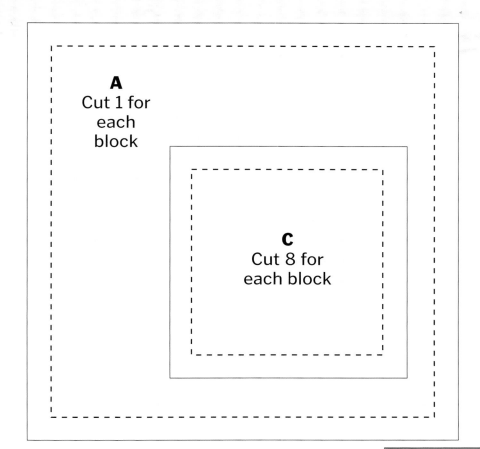

A
Cut 1 for each block

C
Cut 8 for each block

4 inches | 4 inches | 4 inches | 4 inches

C	D	B	D	C
D	C	B	C	D
B		A		B
D	C	B	C	D
C	D	B	D	C

Placement on 12-inch block

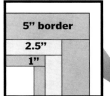

5" border
2.5"
1"

D
Cut 16 for each block

B
Cut 16 for each block

Quilt placement with borders

Starlight Garden

Quilt size 44" x 44"

SUPPLY LIST

- 1/4 yd. each of 4 pink/rose shaded fabrics
- Fat quarter each of 2 pink/rose shaded fabrics
- 1/2 yd. each of 2 burgundy fabrics
- Fat quarter of a large burgundy floral fabric
- 1/2 yd. of 1 green fabric
- 1/4 yd. of 1 green fabric
- Fat quarter each of 2 green fabrics
- 1 yard of a pink check fabric for the center block background
- 1/3 yd. light plaid
- 7/8 yd. light print
- DMC #902, 1 skein

Design by Barb Adams
Appliqué by Leona Adams
Quilting design by Pamela Mayfield

Starlight Garden is a wall sized quilt. These large shapes are forgiving and easy to stitch, presenting a very graphic look!

CENTER BLOCK INSTRUCTIONS:

- Cut the center background square 28 1/2" x 28 1/2" from the light pink check fabric.

- Make plastic templates of all the shapes. Write each template's label and cutting instructions on the template with a Sharpie marker. Keep all the templates together in a plastic zip-lock bag.

- Select templates A through L for the center block.

- Trace around the templates on the right side of your fabric for needle-turn appliqué. Refer to the picture to help with color choice.

- Cut out the shapes, adding your seam allowance.

- Follow the needle-turn appliqué instructions on page 4 and appliqué the pieces to the background.

Placement on a 28-inch square (Enlarge to 400%)

FIRST BORDER:

▪ Cut 2 strips of light fabric 1 1/2" x 28 1/2". Cut 2 strips of light fabric 1 1/2" x 30 1/2".

▪ Cut varying lengths of fabric 1 1/2" wide from burgundy prints. Mix them up and sew 4 strips 1 1/2" x 28 1/2".

▪ With right sides up, lay a burgundy strip on top of a 28" light strip. Baste into place. Repeat for the second 28" light strip. Set aside the remaining strips.

▪ Draw a 1/4" seam allowance along each edge of the strip. Referring to the dogtooth diagram, measure from the seam allowance and mark every two inches along the fabric strip as shown. The marks note the placement of each triangle tip and base.

▪ Begin at the right-hand end of the strip, or if you are left-handed begin on the left end of the strip. Fold under the burgundy fabric from the base up to the tip of the first triangle and appliqué in place. Take an extra stitch to secure the triangle tip.

▪ Refer to the diagram and cut between the first and second triangle. Cut to the seam line. Again, turn under the fabric and appliqué from the tip to the base of the first triangle.

▪ Turn under the fabric for the second triangle and appliqué up to the tip of the triangle. Continue along the strip until all of the dogteeth are appliquéd.

▪ Sew one 28" completed strip to one side of the center block. Repeat the above steps for the opposite side of the center block.

▪ Fold the remaining burgundy and 30" light strips in half to find the centers. With right sides up, align the center of the burgundy strip on top of the center of the light strip. Baste into place. Repeat for the remaining strips. Draw the seam allowances and mark along the strips as before. Appliqué the dogteeth following the previous instructions.

▪ Sew one 30" completed strip to both the top and bottom of the center block.

DOGTOOTH BORDER

Begin your measurements from the 1/4" seam allowance for each side strip.

Clip here

Clip here

1/4" seam allowance

1/4" seam allowance

1/4" seam allowance

SECOND BORDER:
BUTTERFLY BLOCK INSTRUCTIONS:
7 butterfly blocks

- Cut 7 butterfly background squares 6 1/2" x 6 1/2".

- Select templates M, N and O for the butterfly blocks.

- Trace around the templates on the right side of your fabric for needle-turn appliqué. Refer to the picture to help with color choice.

- Cut out the shapes, adding your seam allowance.

- Follow the needle-turn appliqué instructions on page 4 and appliqué the pieces to the background.

- Stem stitch the butterfly detail with DMC #902. Use 6 strands of floss.

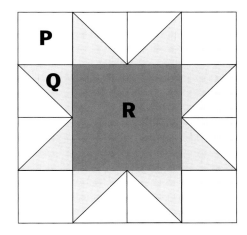

PIECED STAR INSTRUCTIONS:
17 star blocks

- Cut squares 2" x 2" for piece P. Four squares are needed for each block. For 17 star blocks you will need 68 squares.

- Cut squares 2 3/8" x 2 3/8" of contrasting fabric for piece Q. Cut each in half once, on the diagonal. For 17 star blocks you will need to cut 68 light and 68 dark squares in half to form the Q-triangles.

- Sew two contrasting Q-triangles together to form a square. Eight squares are needed for each block. You will need 136 squares total.

- Cut 17 squares 3 1/2" x 3 1/2" for piece R.

- Refer to the sewing diagram and sew 17 pieced star blocks together.

- Refer to the sewing diagram and sew 17 pieced star blocks and 7 butterfly blocks to the center block.

THIRD BORDER:

■ Cut 2 strips of light fabric 1 1/2" x 42 1/2". Cut 2 strips of light fabric 1 1/2" x 44 1/2".

■ Cut varying lengths of fabric 1 1/2" wide from burgundy prints. Mix them up and sew 2 strips 1 1/2" x 42 1/2" and 2 strips 1 1/2" x 44 1/2".

■ With right sides up, lay a 42" burgundy strip on top of a 42" light strip. Baste into place. Repeat for the remaining 42" strips.

■ Draw a 1/4" seam allowance along each edge of the strips. Refer to the dogtooth diagram. Measure from the seam allowance and mark every two inches along the fabric strip as shown. The marks note the placement of each triangle tip and base.

■ Repeat the appliqué instructions used for the first border.

■ Sew one 42 1/2" completed strip to each side of the quilt top.

■ Appliqué both 44" border strips as before and sew one each to the top and bottom of the quilt top.

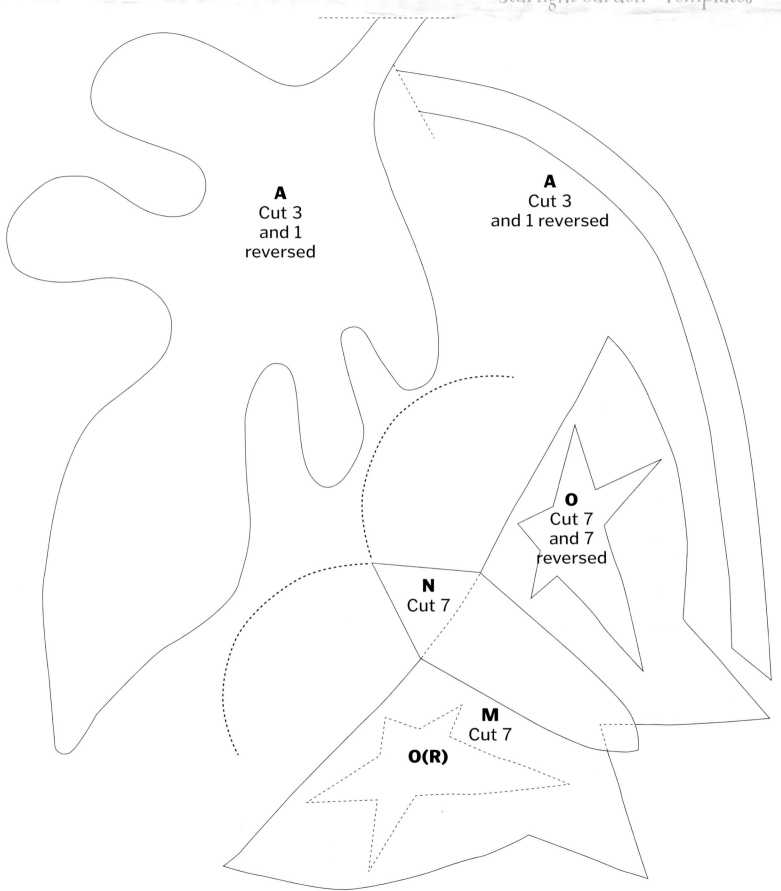

A
Cut 3
and 1
reversed

A
Cut 3
and 1 reversed

O
Cut 7
and 7
reversed

N
Cut 7

M
Cut 7

O(R)

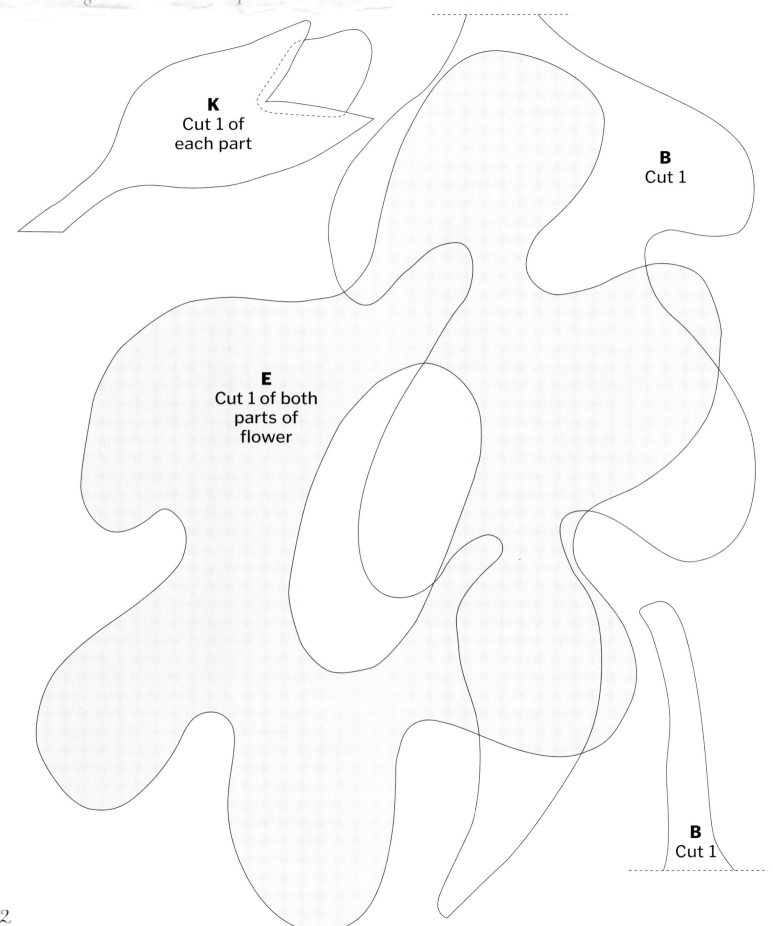

K
Cut 1 of
each part

B
Cut 1

E
Cut 1 of both
parts of
flower

B
Cut 1

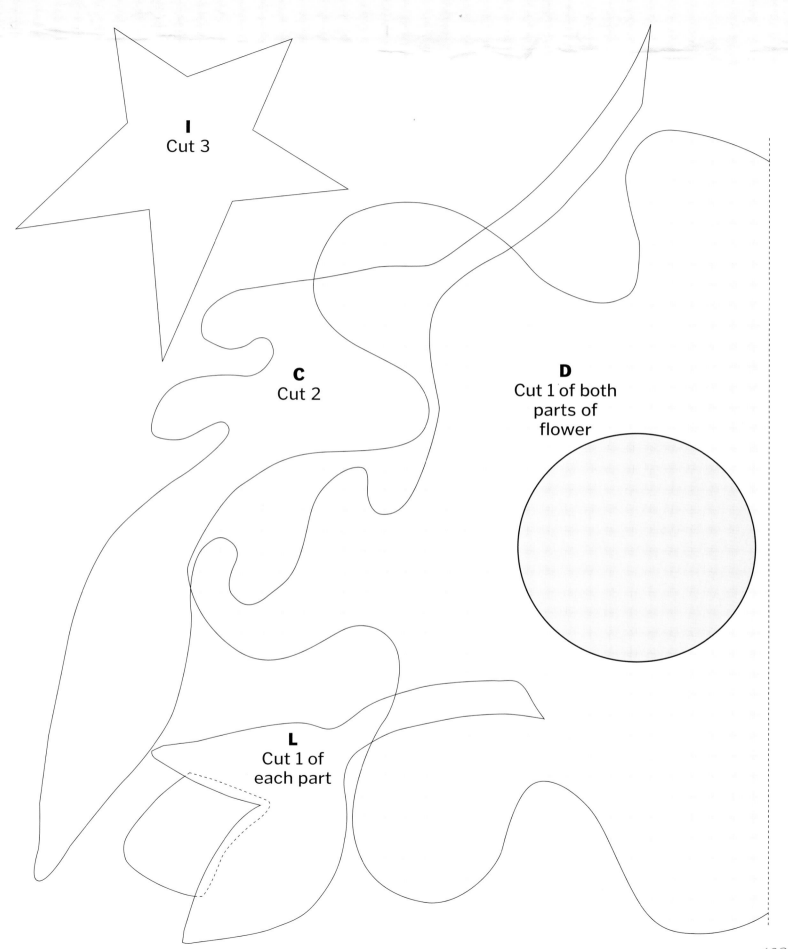

I
Cut 3

C
Cut 2

D
Cut 1 of both
parts of
flower

L
Cut 1 of
each part

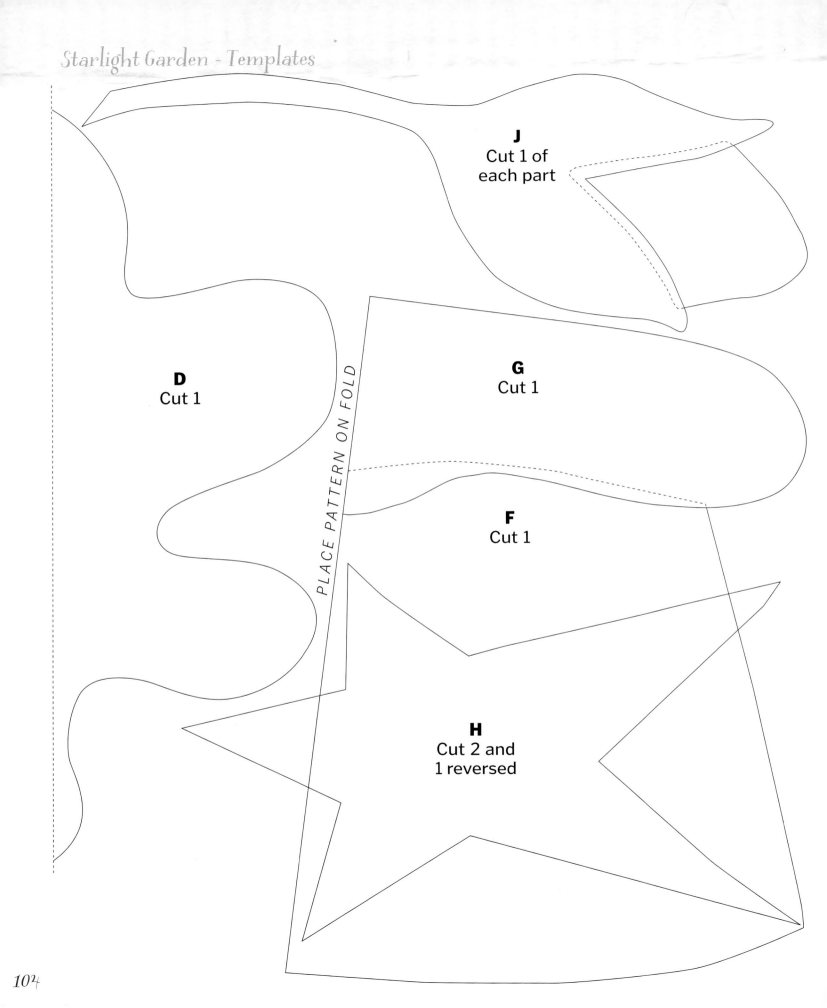

J
Cut 1 of
each part

D
Cut 1

PLACE PATTERN ON FOLD

G
Cut 1

F
Cut 1

H
Cut 2 and
1 reversed

Spring Cottage Hooked Rug

Design by Barb Adams and Alma Allen
Hooked by Alma Allen

Spring Cottage Hooked Rug

Rug Size: 8" x 8"

SUPPLY LIST:

Wool:
- 3" x 18" light olive drab green - leaves, ground and stems
- 3" x 18" antique white - tulips
- 5" x 18" light tan & blue plaid - roof, stepping stone, window trim
- 3" x 18" pale yellow - windows
- 3" x 18" overdyed green & pale orange - leaves, star & flower pot
- 2" x 18" brown - door
- 4" x 18" over-dyed red - house
- 3" x 18" red plaid - house
- 2" x 18" slate grey - chimney
- 3" x 18" light brown check - roof
- Scraps of pink - flower and flower pot
- 4" x 18" each of two different shades of navy - background
- 15" x 15" piece of monk's cloth
- 1 yd. twill tape
- Red Dot tracer or Quilter's Grid by Pellon
- Permanent marking pen (Sharpie fine point)
- Rug frame
- Hook

Any of the featured blocks may be used for a small hooked rug. Use any of the scaled drawings of the featured quilt blocks for a rug pattern. If you would like to make the rug larger, use the copy machine to enlarge the pattern to your desired size.

BASIC INSTRUCTIONS

- Cut your monk's cloth 15" x 15".
- Sew around the edge of the monk's cloth with the zig-zag stitch on your sewing machine to prevent fraying.
- Trace the design to Red Dot tracer.
- Center and transfer the design to your monk's cloth, with your black Sharpie marker.
- Use a #6 blade cut on your wool strips for the rug except for the smaller leaves. A #5 cut was used in the smaller areas to get better detail.
- Outline and hook the shapes first.
- Fill in the background.

After the shapes are filled, begin hooking the background following the contours of the pattern. First, for a smooth appearance, outline all the shapes with the background color. Then, continue to outline the shapes until these outlines begin to meet. Fill the spaces remaining, following a natural flow of hooking.

FINISHING TECHNIQUES

- Dampen a towel and take your finished rug and place it face down on the towel. Iron with a medium steam iron.
- Bind the edges with wool yarn. (I used three strands of navy yarn, chosen to match the navy background and mixed one strand of drab gold yarn with two of light brown yarn to match the drab olive ground.)
- Trim the edges to 1/2" and sew twill tape over the raw edges.

Needlepunch Garden

Design by Barb Adams and Alma Allen

Needlepunched by Alma Allen

Needlepunch Garden

Project Size: 4 1/2" x 4 1/2"

SUPPLY LIST:

- 1/4 yd. Weaver's cloth (available at most craft stores)
- Igolochkoy Russian Punchneedle kit (available at local needlework shops)
- 7" hoop

One each of the following floss skeins are needed for this project:

- GA Butternut Squash- flower center
- GA Melon Patch- flower
- GA Cornhusk- leaves
- WDW Whiskey #2219- four stars
- DMC #732- leaves
- GA Pink Azalea- flower buds
- WDW Pecan #1228- basket
- GA Hyacinth- 2 stars

- Waterlilies by Caron #096 Orange Blossom- background
- Au Ver A Soil #2542- background

(You may substitute 3 skeins of WDW Peach #1131 and 1 skein of WDW Angel Hair #1109 for the background if the silk floss is not available)

This small whimsical design is done with the Igolochkoy Russian Punchneedle tools. The tool kit provides 3 sizes of needles: 1-strand, 3-strand, and 6-strand. Use 3 strands of floss with the 3-strand needle. Follow the needlepunch instructions in the kit to complete this project. The design is worked from the back of the fabric and therefore the pattern is reversed.

- Cut a square of Weaver's cloth 9" x 9".

- Use a light box and trace this design to the reverse side of your cloth with a very fine tipped marker.

- Place your fabric in the hoop and secure very tightly. The pattern should not be distorted in the hoop. Straighten the design as you tighten the fabric in the hoop.

- Outline the shapes and fill with the correct color. Begin with one of the large pink flowers. Fill the center of the flower and then outline the petals and fill. Always needlepunch just inside the drawn line on the fabric, unless you are needlepunching a vine or leaf vein. For a single line of color, needlepunch directly on the drawn line. Clip and trim any longer or loose pieces of floss on the front of the piece. Clip the beginning and ending threads on the back of the piece also.

- Use 1 strand of Cornhusk and 2 strands of #732 for the darker green areas in the leaves and stems. Use 3 strands of Cornhusk for the lighter green areas in the leaves and flower buds.

- Fill in the background last. Use 2 strands of #096 Orange Blossom and 1 strand of Au Ver A Soil #2542.

After the shapes are filled, begin hooking the background following the contours of the pattern. First, for a smooth appearance, outline all the shapes with the background color. Then, continue to outline the shapes until these outlines begin to meet. Fill the spaces remaining, following a natural flow of needlepunch.

Needlepunch Garden pattern

Redwork Pillows

Design by Barb Adams and Alma Allen
Stitching by Leona Adams

Pillow Size: 10" x 10"
SUPPLY LIST:

FOR "SPRING AWAKENING"
- ◼ 1/3 yd. light stripe for the background
- ◼ 1 yd. red fabric for the ruffle and pillow back
- ◼ 2 skeins of DMC floss #3328

FOR "AUTUMN'S HURRAH"
- ◼ 1/3 yd. light print for the background
- ◼ 1 yd. tan fabric for the ruffle and pillow back
- ◼ 1 yd. of another tan print
- ◼ 1 skein of DMC floss #221

FOR BOTH
- ◼ Sulky water soluble stabilizer
- ◼ Sulky fabric temporary spray adhesive
- ◼ 6 oz. Poly-fil

Any of the featured quilt pattern drawings could be used for this redwork pillow design. These pillows feature the patterns from "Spring Awakening" and "Autumn's Hurrah". Choose your favorite and stitch one design to go with your quilt!

INSTRUCTIONS FOR SPRING AWAKENING PILLOW
All cutting measurements include a 1/2" seam allowance. Pattern on page 26.

- ◼ Cut the background block 11" x 11".

- ◼ Cut pillow backing 12" x 12" and set aside.

- ◼ Trace the design to the Sulky water soluble stabilizer.

- ◼ Spray the back of the stabilizer with Sulky temporary fabric-spray adhesive. Center and position the stabilizer on the top of the background block.

- ◼ Stem-stitch the design with 3 strands of DMC #3328 floss using a large eye embroidery needle.

- ◼ Stitch the berries and leaves with the satin-stitch or use Leona's method. Leona uses the button-hole stitch, which frames and fills the motif.

- ◼ Cut away most of the stabilizer from the design when the stitching is completed. Remove the stabilizer from the design following the product instructions.

■ Cut 7" wide bias strips and sew them together for the ruffle. You will need about 120" length for the ruffle.

■ Fold the ruffle in half lengthwise, wrong sides together and press.

■ Gather the ruffle. With right sides together, pin the ruffle to the pillow top. While pinning, ease the gathered ruffle evenly around the pillow top.

■ Sew the ruffle to the pillow top.

■ Sew the pillow front to the pillow back right sides together. Use a 1/2" seam allowance. Leave a 4" opening on the bottom seam for turning.

■ Turn and stuff with poly-fil. Blind stitch the opening closed.

INSTRUCTIONS FOR "AUTUMN'S HURRAH"
All cutting measurements include a 1/2" seam allowance. Pattern on page 52.

■ Refer to "Spring's Awakening" pillow for cutting and transfer instructions.

■ Stem-stitch the design with 3 strands of DMC #221 floss using a large eye embroidery needle.

■ Cut 7" wide bias strips and sew them together for the first ruffle. You will need about 120" length for the ruffle.

■ Fold the ruffle in half lengthwise, wrong sides together and press.

■ Gather the ruffle. With right sides together, pin the ruffle to the pillow top. While pinning, ease the gathered ruffle evenly around the pillow top.

■ Cut 9" wide bias strips and sew them together for the outside ruffle. You will need about 120" length for the ruffle.

■ Again, fold the ruffle in half lengthwise, wrong sides together and press and gather.

■ Baste both ruffles to the pillow top.

■ Sew the pillow front to the pillow back, right sides together. Use a 1/2" seam allowance. Leave a 5" opening on the bottom seam for turning.

■ Turn and stuff with poly-fil. Blind stitch the opening closed.

Chocolate & Flowers

Design by Pamela Mayfield and Barb Adams

Quilting design by Lori Kukuk

Appliqué by Pamela Mayfield and Jean Stanclift

Chocolate & Flowers

SUPPLY LIST

Quilt size: 64" x 64"

■ 2 1/4 yd. chocolate brown stripe - background and binding

■ 2 yds. chocolate brown print - sashing and border

■ Fat quarter each of 4 red fabrics for the containers

■ Fat quarter each of 4 green prints for bias stems

■ Add scraps of greens for leaves

■ Fat quarter of 5 blue fabrics for berries, stars and border squares

■ Fat quarter of a yellow batik for flowers

■ 1/2 yd. yellow for first border

P am chose four blocks from the featured quilt to use for this dramatic quilt. The bright colors "pop" when placed on this dark chocolate background. Pam's blocks are Hearts of Spring, Spring Awakening, Summer's Herbs and Autumn's Hurrah (see index). Chose your favorite four blocks from the featured quilt to reproduce Pam's quilt.

INSTRUCTIONS
All cutting measurements include
a 1/4" seam allowance.

■ Pick four blocks from the featured quilt section of the book. Refer to the picture to assist with color placement and appliqué the shapes into place.

■ Cut 2 strips of dark sashing fabric 2 1/4" x 20 1/2".

■ Cut 1 strip of dark sashing fabric 2 1/4" x 42 1/4".

■ Refer to the diagram and sew the blocks together.

FIRST BORDER

■ Cut 2 strips of dark fabric 2 1/8" x 42 1/4". Sew one strip to each side of the quilt top.

■ Cut 2 strips of dark fabric 2 1/8" x 45 1/2". Sew one strip each to the top and bottom of the quilt top.

SECOND BORDER

- Cut 64 blue squares 2 5/8" x 2 5/8" for piece C.
- Cut 30 yellow squares 4 1/4" x 4 1/4". Cut each square in half twice on the diagonal for piece B.

- Cut 4 yellow squares 3" x 3". Cut each square in half on the diagonal once for piece A.

- Sew 1 blue square and 2 yellow triangles together to form one border unit. Refer to the diagram.

- Sew 2 strips of 15 units each.

- Sew small triangles to square up border strips. Use one for the inside corners and one for the outside corners.

- Sew one unit strip to each side of the quilt top.

- Sew 2 strips of 17 units each.

- Sew small triangles to square up border strips. Use one for the inside corners and one for the outside corners.

- Sew one unit strip each to the top and bottom of the quilt top.

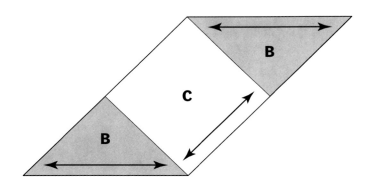

SEW BORDER UNITS TOGETHER TO FORM THE SECOND BORDER.

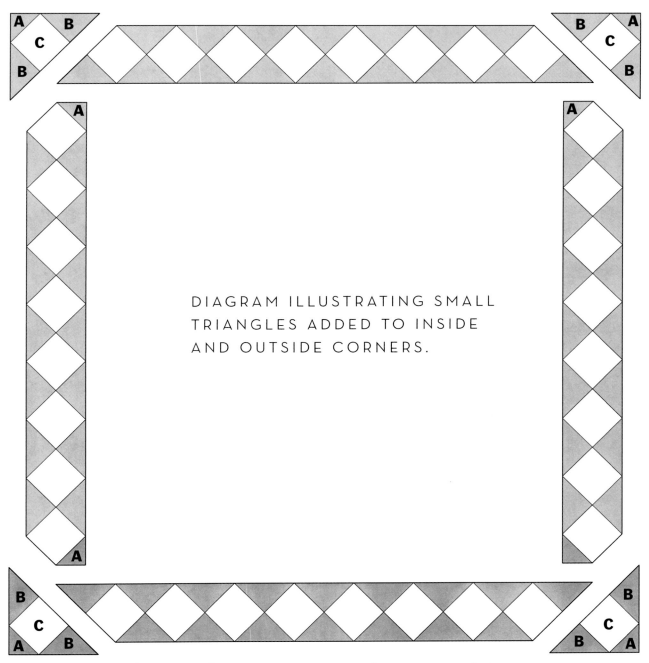

DIAGRAM ILLUSTRATING SMALL
TRIANGLES ADDED TO INSIDE
AND OUTSIDE CORNERS.

NOTE: diagram does not reflect an accurate count of pieces - see photo on page 114.

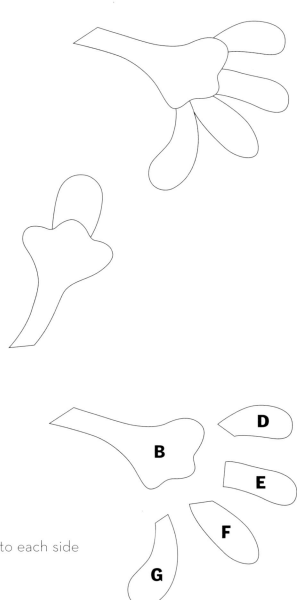

PAM ADDED FLOWERS TO HER
SUMMER HERB BLOCK. WE'RE
INCLUDING THOSE TEMPLATES
FOR YOU.

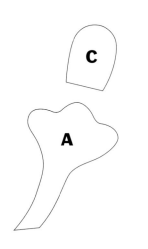

THIRD BORDER

◼ Cut 2 strips of dark fabric 6 3/4" x 51 1/2". Sew one strip to each side of the quilt top.

◼ Cut 2 strips of dark fabric 6 3/4" x 64". Sew one strip each to the top and bottom of the quilt top.

◼ Make 4 feet of 1/2" bias vine. Cut leaves and berries from your favorite featured pattern. Refer to the picture and appliqué the vine, leaves and berries in a whimsical fashion to the corners of two borders.

2¹/₈" x 45¹/₂"

2¹/₄" x 20¹/₂"

2¹/₈" x 42¹/₄"

2¹/₄" x 42¹/₄"

2¹/₈" x 42¹/₄"

2¹/₄" x 20¹/₂"

2¹/₈" x 45¹/₂"

NOTE: diagram does not reflect an accurate count of pieces - see photo on page 114.

Peppermint & Holly

Designed by Barb Adams

Appliqué by Leona Adams

Quilting Design by Jeanne Zyck

Peppermint & Holly

Quilt size: 70" x 70"
SUPPLY LIST

- 4 1/2 yds. light print for the background
- 1 yd. each of two red fabrics
- 1/4 yd. large red floral print
- 1 yd. green print
- 1/2 yd. each of two green prints

 diagram A

 diagram B

Barb's quilt is embellished with winter spirit. The candy cane frame and holly leaf border make this quilt a special treat to use all winter long. Barb used the blocks Winter Haven and Winter Bloom from the featured quilt. She changed the color scheme, added a new border and the results are a new look for these designs!

INSTRUCTIONS:

All cutting measurements include a 1/4" seam allowance.

- Refer to pages 6 and 12 for block instructions. Refer to the picture for color placement and appliqué four blocks.

- Cut 265 squares 2 1/2" x 2 1/2" from the light background print.

- Cut 265 squares 2 1/2" x 2 1/2" from the red fabrics.

- Place one red square and one light square right sides together. Sew a seam along the diagonal as illustrated in diagram A.

- Trim away the excess fabric as illustrated in diagram B. Open the triangle units and press.

- Refer to the diagram on page 122 and sew 6 strips of 10 units each.
- Refer to the diagram on page 122 and sew 3 strips of 23 units each.
- Lay the strips and blocks out to visualize the sewing sequence. Refer to the diagram and sew the quilt top together.

- Save the remaining units for the second border.

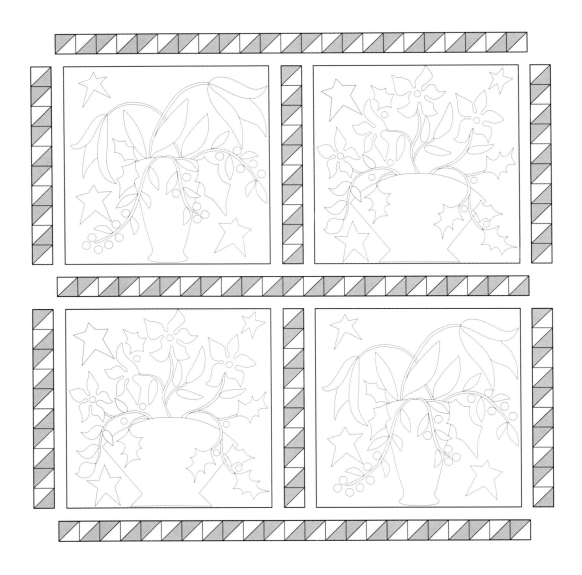

Peppermint & Holly

FIRST BORDER

■ Cut 2 strips of light fabric 10 1/2" x 46 1/2". Sew one to each side of the quilt top.

■ Cut 2 strips of light fabric 10 1/2" x 66 1/2". Sew one each to the top and bottom of the quilt top.

■ Cut 16 and 16R of piece F located with the 'Winter Haven' templates on page 10 (large holly leaf)

■ Cut 8 of piece H located with the 'Winter Haven' templates on page 11 (small holly leaf)

■ Cut 20 of piece L located with the 'Winter Haven' templates on page 10 (berry)

■ Make 8 yards of 1/4" bias vine from green fabric.

■ Refer to the picture and whimsically lay the vine, leaves and berries along the borders. Baste the shapes in place and then appliqué.

SECOND BORDER

■ Sew 2 strips of 33 units each. Refer to the picture for placement of the units. Sew one strip to each side of the quilt top.

■ Sew 2 strips of 35 units each. Refer to the picture for placement of the units. Sew one strip to both the top and bottom of the quilt top.

Kansas City Star Quilt Books

Notes:

Notes:

Notes: